MW01254401

*A*N *I*NTR*O*DUCTION to *G*NOSTIC *H*ᴱBREW *Q*ABBᴬL

Murray Webber

Seven Oaks Publishing

An Introduction to Gnostic Hebrew Qabbal, by Murray Webber.
© 1995 Seven Oaks Press, Toronto. All rights reserved. Printed in Canada.
No part of this book may be used or reproduced in any manner whatsoever
without written permission except in the case of brief quotations embodied in
critical articles and reviews. For additional information address:
595A Church St #4, Toronto, Ontario, Canada M4Y 2E6

CANADIAN CATALOGUING IN PUBLICATION DATA

Webber, Murray, 1929–
    An Introduction to Gnostic Hebrew Qabbal

    Includes bibliographical references.
    ISBN 0-9699446-0-8

    1. Cabala.   2. Mysticism – Judaisim.   I. Title

BM526.W43   1995
296.1'6   C95-931311-7

Table of Contents

Foreword

The purpose of this book is to create a deeper understanding of
certain aspects of what is termed the Gnostic Hebrew Qabbal, as
a guidepost to those who wish to study a distinctly Western style
of personal spiritual liberation. The word Gnostic is borrowed
from the Greek *gnosis* meaning knowledge, or more precisely,
divinely inspired knowledge, which is its present day definition.
This knowledge is largely reflected in mankind's conscious and
subconscious relationship with Nature in its broadest possible
cosmic sense. A great deal of information concerning what some
term The Qabbalah has been buried under the guise of secret
teachings, hidden knowledge and downright superstition for an
even greater variety of reasons.

   Scholars have generally grouped studies of these teachings
under the heading of Jewish Mysticism. However there exist
many different interpretations of its significance in terms of its
historic development and scope. For example, there are quite a
number of early texts of an esoteric nature that were written over
the past thousand years. Yet it is nearly impossible to find written
evidence of the initial oral tradition (as was so common in those
times, owing to the common lack of literacy or formal education,
to give one reason) that it is said to go back many more thousands
of years – *beyond the time of recorded memory.*

What is presented here is meant to be taken in the most universal sense possible, devoid of any restrictions as to race, creed, colour, age, sex, or any other barriers that have been placed upon the dissemination of higher knowledge, or its use.

About the author...
Murray Webber was born and continues to reside in Toronto, Canada, one of the main metaphysical centres of North America. He taught Gnostic Hebrew Qabbal for over a decade in both formal and informal sessions in such diverse settings as the Theosophical Society and the Unity Church. His students come from many backgrounds and religious traditions, which is in keeping with a teaching that does not favour any particular race, creed, colour or sex.

Mr. Webber has travelled extensively and has studied with such noted Western and Eastern spiritual teachers as Leslie Dawson, His Holiness The Gwyala Karmapa, and Karma Thinley Rinpoche. These and many other Eastern and Western masters of inner teachings and meditation have fostered a prodigious understanding and experience of the meeting of metaphysical hemispheres.

This is Mr. Webber's first book — an unprecedented unravelling of the Hebrew symbols and an introduction to Gnostic themes that are universal in scope. In his own words: "I don't teach speculation — only things that I have personally experienced."

Introduction

The Hebrew alphabet is comprised of twenty-two symbols, three of which are designated "mothers", seven are called "doubles", and twelve are "singles"[1] . The mothers are major gates of purification; the doubles are dualities of states of consciousness; and singles are singular in the sense of fixed and difficult states of mind. As an example of a double, the symbol Kaf כ has the meaning of both nourishment and the absence of nourishment. All of the symbols have a vast metaphysical significance that reaches far beyond the usual associations with written communications.

For those who have little or no experience of the Hebrew symbols, they are read from right to left, as are the words and sentences they form. They are also used to designate numbers. It is also notable that when these symbols are used for common linguistic purposes, they are actually classified as consonants. When one examines a printed Hebrew text, one will note that various diacritical marks appear above and below the actual symbols: these represent vowels, guides to syllabic emphasis, and runs of musical notes. The earliest Hebrew writings were devoid of these markings, which invariably meant that the correct pronunciation of words (in fact any kind of comprehensive reading) or the singing of the Hebrew Scriptures was reserved for those who had access to knowledgeable teachers. Within the symbols lies a rich and varied tapestry of shades of meaning that encompass the entirety of Creation. And still, there is an ongoing evolutionary process that continues to weave even more splendid patterns within the fabric of this knowledge that belongs to all times, from the distant past to the present, and into the future.

What follows is an illumination of some of the aspects of these symbols, which have long been referred to as the "Sacred Letters from Heaven". For countless centuries it has been asserted that the symbols were an operational vehicle for the coming into existence of Creation itself, which lies within the realm of ontology (the study of being: from the Greek, *ontos*, being, and *logos*, discourse). In fact, it has been suggested that the twenty-two Hebrew symbols were not originally created as a linguistic tool, but rather were the outcome of the meditation experiences of the ancient Hebrew Sages, who in turn wrote the Hebrew Scriptures. As such, they have individual meanings that transcend their everyday use as agents of language alone.

Moreover, Hebrew Scriptures themselves can be interpreted beyond the usual historical or suggestive level, and attain a more universal value in terms of their significance in relation to mankind's ongoing search for insight into the meaning of all life on earth and the cosmic universes.

The historical stories employed by the ancient Hebrew Sages contain deep allegories and metaphors that hide significant inner meanings.

It is part of an ancient tradition that springs from the Hebrew word "makbil" מַקְבִּל which appears only once in Scriptures (EX XXVI:5), and means parallel. Other companion meanings include: to give and to receive, cause and effect, opposite, similar, oscillating, compare, contrast, and preservation. All twenty-two Hebrew symbols form multiple levels of metaphysical circles, with the beginning symbols meeting the last in an ongoing, infinite pattern that mirrors the highest aspects of metaphysical teachings anywhere, from any time.

One of the underpinnings of Rabbinical Judaism is that the God referred to in the Hebrew Scriptures is the God of the Jewish people. However, Gnostic Hebrew Qabbal teaching maintains that there is a *single imageless Creator* beyond the conventional God or Lord.

Mysticism has often been defined as a search for direct contact with the divine. Questions about the origins of life and other related themes are not dependent upon any specific form of religious thought. Inquiries of this nature apply to all humanity, and have persisted through all ages. It is interesting to note that most major civilizations have contributed to the development of such philosophic trends – even the very terminology utilized to express the intellectual manifestations of what exists beyond logic and sense perception. Mankind's quest for knowledge and understanding have never been limited to avenues of the expressly tangible. However only a statistically small percentage of any given population pursues such areas of exploration (even in the more conventional disciplines, such as the physical sciences).

Readers who are familiar with other schools of metaphysical contemplation will find a great deal of common ground . Any complete teaching must approach Truth from the point of view that it applies to all forms of life without regard to geographical, ethnic, sexual, spatial, or chronologic distinctions.

At the same time, it is the writer's intention to provide as much explanation as possible for those who may have little previous experience with esoteric themes.

It is not possible, nor is it even desirable, to attempt to codify or explain *everything*. That is the work that is best left to the motivated reader or student. It is also emphasized that those who are sufficiently motivated to pursue this study in any depth, find an experienced teacher who is capable of directing them .

Gnostic Hebrew Qabbal teaching is not an "ism", religion or organized movement, but *a Path* that leads to Personal Discovery of Man's Relationship with his Soul, Nature and the single imageless Creator as revealed in Hebrew Scriptures. It is a Path that can lead an individual to peace and tranquility through Love and Compassion, Wisdom and Understanding. It is a Path comprised of metaphysics and meditation. It might best be summed up by the statement, "Don't take my word for it, experience it!" This is in keeping with the orientation of the Western mind that does not traditionally bend itself to "do what you're told". In order for one to discover the treasures inherent in this teaching, one will find that there must be a meeting of the intellectual (left brain) and intuitive (right brain) sides of the mind.

In addition to the metaphysical interpretation of the Hebrew symbols, this book contains several sections dealing with overviews of major themes in Gnostic Hebrew Qabbal teachings. These have been included so that the reader may have a closer look at how the symbols, and their significance, relate to the very broad scope that these studies entail. (See Chapter I).

It is a distinct social commentary on the part of modern Western society that since the early 1960's there has been an enormous mental movement towards spirituality in a variety of forms. It is our hope that this work will shed some light on a teaching that has not received a great deal of exposure, but is not "new" by any stretch of the imagination. The total study and practice can be revealed through the stories and events of Hebrew Scriptures, plus the revelations of the twenty-two Hebrew symbols and their relationship with colour, sound and geometry.

It is intended that this book become the catalyst that ignites a greater illumination...

---

[1] As defined in the Sepher Yetsirah (Book of Creation), about which more information is provided later in the text.

The Hebrew Symbols

א	Aleph	ל	Lahmed
ב	Beth	מ	Mem
ג	Gimmel	נ	Nun
ד	Daleth	ס	Samekh
ה	Hé	ע	A'yin
ו	Vav	פ	Pé
ז	Zayin	צ	Tzadi
ח	Het	ק	Qof
ט	Teth	ר	Resh
י	Yod	שׁ	Shin
כ	Kaf	ת	Tav

Final letters
The following are used to end a Hebrew word

ך	Kaf	ף	Pé
ם	Mem	ץ	Tzadi
ן	Nun		

Definitions & Themes in Gnostic Hebrew Qabbal Teaching

Today the Hebrew word "Qabbal"[2] (usually spelled with a "c" or "k" in English) is rather misunderstood. The original meaning has been watered down to the point where it hardly resembles that of even a few years ago.

The "Path of the Holy Breath" has its foundation in the original Hebrew Qabbal teachings. It is based on the metaphysical interpretation of Hebrew Scriptures and the practice of meditation.

Before proceeding to the definitions, a few words are perhaps in order on what is meant by "metaphysical" and how its meanings are derived and utilized.

Metaphysics expresses ideas as concrete objects as well as abstractions, and the two functions should not be confused. Many people find the abstract difficult to comprehend, because abstractions do not have physical *referents*. We commonly use abstractions in everyday language without thinking too deeply about them: concepts like love, for example, or statements that try to capture an essence – "It's *like* this..." The language of the abstract tends to be metaphorical; it attempts to approximate things (and even more intellectually mind-bending, non-things) by using symbols that inasmuch say, "It's like this..."

Where metaphysics tends to boggle the intellect, the intuitive, meditative mind has the capacity to "unravel" the meanings behind the symbols. In terms of deep, inner teachings, certain concepts cannot be expressed in language at all; the words simply haven't been invented, or *cannot* be created, because the "things" that one would like to describe cannot be described. Rather they must be experienced. One can only have some vague notion about infinity for example, which cannot readily be demonstrated. Often, metaphysics has to resort to defining its terms by explaining what something is not. If one cannot describe what something is, the opposite approach might be more fruitful.

Interestingly enough, some of us find the study of metaphysics exciting and fun. In any event, it is a fair statement to also say that the in-depth study of inner teachings is not easy. Very often it leads one into wrong turns, backtracking, traps, curves and dead ends. If one is persistent, however, and imbued with a sense of adventure, one will find that it encompasses more challenges than any computer game or equivalent pursuit. One ancient piece of wisdom states that one will find what one is searching for when one is ready to receive it. It is not a matter of blind faith, but an honest quest for discovery. One will see if one really wants to, but one must also have focus and direction.

Qabbal

A very long time ago, Qabbal was used to describe only the inner, abstract Hebrew teaching. Now, it describes any occult, mystical, secret doctrine or science. A simplified definition is: "The study and practice of man's relationship with the soul and nature."

The correct three symbol form קבל may be found in Hebrew in the Five Books of Moses in DAN VI:1, VII:18, JOB II:10, ESTH IX:27 and I-CH. XII:18. The original form of the Hebrew word Qabbal may be found in EX XXVI:5, and XXXVI:12, where it is spelled with five symbols מקביל. In this context, it can mean both parallel and opposite at the same time. We shall search for its meaning using the more familiar three symbol word, which in its simplest sense, means to receive, to take, origin and sometimes tradition.

To reach the inner meaning one has to move beyond common language and linear, analytical interpretations. Try to understand the words and symbols in the metaphysical sense, on a dimensionless, abstract plane.

As one moves deeper into the metaphysics of these three symbols קבל, one finds a sense of reflection and learning that combines both intellectual thought and intuition. Qabbal is received by way of insight and revelation. It means being taught and guided as well as by personal self-discovery. This self-illumination is a constant urging forward of oneself to attain a state of balanced harmony with love, compassion, wisdom and understanding. In short, it is a raising of the spiritual consciousness.

Qabbal teaching could also be defined as:

> "Receiving the origins of a transcendental teaching through instruction and self-illumination."

Here the word transcendental becomes a metaphor for soul and nature.

Hebrew

The word Hebrew is noted here in its context with the teaching of *Ruach Ha Kodesh* (The Path of the Holy Breath) which has its roots in the Hebrew Qabbal.

In approaching the inner meaning of the word Hebrew let us examine the concept of monotheism, which was scripturally attributed to Abram. This is the belief and faith in a single imageless Creator – a single, imageless God who creates us (rather than the other way around). The great philosopher Montaigne stated, "Man is stark raving mad. He cannot make a worm, but he makes gods by the dozen!".

The word *Hebrew* is used in Scriptures for the first time in GEN XIV:13, as an adjective to describe Abram. The symbols in Hebrew are עברי and the correct pronunciation is "e-vree". He passed over, or transcended the mythological river Eber עֵבֶר and discovered the revelation of a single imageless Creator. The literal meaning of the word is *belonging to Eber*. Hebrew mythology declares that Eber was the name of a river that one has to cross to enter the path of monotheism, or to enter the Hebrew path. Hebrew may then be defined as:

> "The monotheistic concept whereby man can raise himself out of a scattered materialistic state of mind and transcend or pass over to the higher concept of a single imageless Creator."

Hebrew Qabbal may also be defined as:

> "The study and practice of man's relationship with his soul, nature, and the single imageless Creator as revealed in the Sacred Hebrew Scriptures."

In accordance with the above, the ability to cross over is not limited to any one race, creed, colour or sex.

Gnostic Hebrew Qabbal is very ancient, going back beyond living memory. "Ruach Ha Kodesh" or "Holy Breath" or "Holy Spirit" is the name that this particular Hebrew Qabbal teaching is known by. The last time it was taught openly was about 1500 years ago. It went underground, so to speak, when the Catholic Church and the Jewish Rabbinate drove metaphysics from their canonized teachings.[3]

Since that time, the teaching has been passed from teacher to disciple, by word of mouth. The writer received the keys of Ruach Ha Kodesh from his teacher, Leslie Dawson, a living master of Western and Eastern teachings.

The "Path of the Holy Breath" is the study and practice of metaphysical Hebrew Scriptures and their meditations.

The path has stood the test of time, and comes from a rich and ancient heritage. It is named after the first of seven main meditation techniques which man has practiced since time immemorial:

1. Breathing
2. Energy Centres
3. Visualization
4. Sound
5. Movement
6. Devotion
7. Insight

This teaching does not assert that it is the only path to Truth or Spiritual Awareness. It does not teach that one accept the words of the teacher as gospel. There are many honourable paths, and one should seek out the path most comfortable to one's self. Self-discovery is vital. Only through self-discovery can one establish whether or not a particular teaching contains the Truth.

Metaphysical

The term is comprised of two words, *meta* and *physical.* Meta expresses the idea of transcending, passing over, or going beyond. Physical is a linear concept in terms of tangible objects. When the two words are combined, they become an expression of transcending or going beyond the physical. One can then move one's state of consciousness from the common linear/analytical to the dimensionless/abstract – in other words from the conscious to the subconscious. *Metaphysical* does not have the same depth of meaning as the Hebrew word *Qabbal.* In placing these abstract terms into word form there is no intention that these common metaphors create in any form a graven image of the ineffable Creator.

The term metaphysical may be further defined as the study and practice of transforming/transcending the physical. We can also combine the definitions of Hebrew and metaphysics so that Hebrew Metaphysics is "The study and practice of the transcendental through the Hebrew Qabbal".

One may also see the term Western Mysteries used. These may be thought of as "Multiple combinations of concealed Western teachings".

Graven images & idolatry

Graven images are first mentioned in EX xx:4 of the Hebrew Scriptures: "Thou shalt not make unto thee a graven image, nor any manner of likeness, of anything that is in heaven above, or that is in the earth beneath, or that is in the water under the earth". The example that comes to most minds is found in EX XXXII:1-6, in which the children of Israel have Aaron fashion a molten golden calf while waiting for Moses who was on Mount Sinai. Once again we find in EX XXXIV:17, "Thou shalt make thee no molten gods". In LEV XIX:4 we find "Turn ye not unto the idols, nor make to yourselves molten gods: I am the Lord your God".

Consequently, graven images/idolatry may be defined as:

> "The product of wishful, scattered thoughts that become fashioned into an object, or objects of adulation or worship".

Metaphors

Inner teachings that come from the West or the Occident tend to be hidden in metaphors or allegories. Hebrew Scriptures are similar. Teachings that come from the East (Orient) tend to state their case more openly. The ancient Hebrew Sages hid the secret teachings in metaphors, fables, parables and allegories.

Almost 60 years ago, the Unity Church of Truth produced a competent *Metaphysical Bible Dictionary* of the proper names and places which appear in both Hebrew and Christian Scriptures. Common words also have esoteric meanings. The simple word cattle, which we usually consider to be old-fashioned, is an example. It can be found about 125 times in Hebrew Scriptures. Metaphysically, it means thoughtless followers. The abstract idea expressed is that of a herd of mindless creatures guided by mob psychology.

Virtually all the Hebrew Scriptures contain these metaphors. When properly interpreted, they are a guide to raising one's state of spiritual consciousness. When correctly understood, they erase the inconsistencies of which Hebrew Scriptures are so often accused.

A metaphor may be defined as:

> "A word or statement that creates an illusion, an object of reference, while hiding the true meaning".

Hebrew symbols

In Hebrew Qabbal teaching, the symbols were used by the Ancient Sages to keep the four levels of teaching intact:

1   Historical
2.   Suggestive
3.   Inner
4.   Innermost

These are the link between earth, the cosmic universe and the Creator: the contact between the formed and the unformed. This is why the Hebrew symbols are often referred to as the Sacred Letters from Heaven, and the Voice of the Creator.

Intellectually, these symbols are a means of communication that enable us to read, speak and hear the historical teachings. Intuitively and meditatively, they serve as guides to the inner and innermost teachings. Through study and practice, they can lead the individual directly to the summit of Hebrew Qabbal teaching.

Originally, Hebrew Scriptures were written with no breaks between the words. An unbroken sequence of approximately 20-30 symbols were written on each line – just enough for one breath. Parts of the Torah (the Five Books of Moses) are still printed in this way. Examples of lines with no breaks may be found in GEN II:21, GEN XIV:13 in the Hebrew. One can find others with little effort. These are not misprints or accidents – they were purposely left unchanged by the ancient Hebrew Sages to remind us of the original intent of the printed word.

It is suggested that the Hebrew Scriptures were written in this way as they were meant only for the few in the priesthood who were privy to their inner meaning. As time went on, the number of followers increased, and it became necessary to interpret the teachings on a broader level, while at the same time preserving the secrecy of the inner meanings. The inner and innermost teachings formed the basis of the suggestive teachings. From this came the historical story.

To this day, the order of Hebrew symbols cannot be altered or modified. This protects the innermost/hidden teaching – the Hebrew Qabbal. Modernists, who are not aware of this, quite rightly in fact, observe that the stories are not only outdated, but also inconsistent. In many instances they seem to make no sense.

This is because the prescribed order of symbols, when interpreted on a purely historical basis, force these stories to go "tilt" from time to time. Yet this is a small price to pay in order to maintain the integrity of a rich heritage.

The Hebrew symbols are far more than an alphabet or means of communication. The form as we know it today evolved from the Hebrew Sages' meditation experiences. Only at a later date did they become an alphabet. If the themes used in Hebrew Scriptures were expressed openly in abstract concepts, they would not be understood by the vast majority. In fact, the quaint, anti-quated words are not arbitrary; they were carefully chosen to create metaphors and symbols.

The ultimate accomplishment of the study and practice of the Hebrew Qabbal is a mind that is balanced: the balanced harmony of love, compassion, wisdom and understanding. This will lead the individual to *unity* with the single imageless Creator, or, as expressed in other teachings, as enlightenment or as a full awakening.

The Hebrew Scriptures, expressed as an historical story, speak in the common language. The terms are borrowed from human concepts and the empirical world. These terms can easily lead one into fantasy, scattered emotions, misdirected concepts and idolatry.

Man

The historical interpretation of the word "man" in all scriptural teachings is badly misunderstood. In the inner or Hebrew Qabbal teaching, the word man is a metaphor for *humanity* as a whole. It is not a synonym for the word "male". Different Hebrew words are used to delineate female, woman, male and man.

Too often the transition to another language does not do justice to the specific word, and occasionally words are taken out of context. This results in the original inner Hebrew meaning being lost or misinterpreted. This results in what is called *false knowledge.*

When a distinction of the sexes in their physical form is

being made in Hebrew Scriptures, the only Hebrew words used
are:

נְקֵבָה   Nekevah   female

זָכָר   Zakhar   male

When they stand by themselves, their meaning is also quite
clear.

The word for man/mankind, in Hebrew, is commonly pronounced *Adam* אָדָם. It never appears with the word in Hebrew
for male. It was *never* meant to denote the male gender.

When the Hebrew Sages wished to distinguish between the
metaphysical anima (female) and animus (male), they used the
words "man" אִישׁ and "woman" אִשָּׁה.

Sacrifice

The normal historical understanding of the word *sacrifice* in
Hebrew Scriptures is *to kill*. The word can also mean *offer*, or *a
gift*. In metaphysical terms it means destruction, weakening, or
fading. Its main meaning in Hebrew Qabbal teaching is: "The
weakening or fading of unwholesome states and conditions of
consciousness".

Burnt offerings

Metaphysically, burnt offerings are a divine function which
expresses that which goes up. This theme also contains the
abstract thought or action of a humble or contrite heart.
Making a burnt offering is:

> "A means of transcending one's animal consciousness and the
> body substance to a higher state."

This refining process usually takes place in stages.
Consequently, many sacrifices and burnt offerings are required.

Sheep

This word is the metaphor for thoughts that automatically and
without question obey the laws of Nature. It is a state of consciousness that is pure and innocent. This is very positive. In fact,

this is the main thought we have of sheep. They are faithful, soft and will conform. They submit easily.

What one thinks of as being a plus in sheep actually hides a dark side of consciousness, a barrier to raising one's spiritual being. This blind, sweet obedience hides ignorance, which keeps us from the Truth. It keeps us backward and unaware. It keeps us in a constant state of not knowing. It is this state of not knowing that the Hebrew Scriptures teach us to sacrifice.

Light

The concept of light in Hebrew Qabbal teaching is too vast to be expanded in this short work. The following metaphysical explanations are basic:

> Creation is the direct result of white light.
>
> Light creates consciousness and colour.
>
> Colour creates form.
>
> Light is consciousness.
>
> Light and consciousness are inseparable.
>
> Light, when used wholesomely, can lift consciousness up from oblivion.
>
> Light can raise spiritual consciousness.
>
> The Light of Creation goes beyond the accepted laws of modern day science and physics.
>
> Without the theme of creative White Light *(Ain-Soph)* or the energy centres *(Sephiroth)*, there would be no Hebrew Qabbal.

Colour

It is through colour that form takes place. In the Hebrew Qabbal, colour is the theme for the *Mind of God.*

Gates of Purification

The Gates of Purification are reminiscent of all that is evoked by a gate or door. They symbolize the transition from one realm to another, or from one realm to the next, and are often referred to as the "heavenly gates". In many teachings, the great gates lead to the world beyond life/death. A closed door infers that there is a hidden secret, whereas an open door allows one to pass through to discover the secret. The door is a feminine symbol that denotes a move to varying states of consciousness.

Purification denotes the action of cleansing, refining and ultimately, the liberation of spiritual powers that are capable of transmuting the body, speech and mind into their divine essences or realms.

What has been presented here is by no means a complete or exhaustive study, but rather an introductive illustration of how Gnostic Hebrew Qabbal definitions and themes are expanded from the literal Scriptural stories. The motivated reader may work out the expanded meanings of other Hebrew Scriptural words and themes by referencing the following: an accredited Biblical Concordance, a Thesaurus (Roget's is recommended as it is laid out in a metaphysical fashion), and a Metaphysical Bible Dictionary.

---

[2] The English equivalents of the Hebrew Symbols follow that used in the Complete English-Hebrew Dictionary by Reuben Alcalay (published by Massada Publishing Co., Ramat Gan-Jerusalem, Israel), with one exception: the author has chosen the nineteenth Hebrew symbol Kuf ק instead of the more commonly accepted eleventh Hebrew symbol Kaph כ in the English transliteration of this word, so as to more closely identify with the origins of the word Qabbal in Hebrew Scriptures.

[3] Between the time of the second destruction of the Temple in Jerusalem and 500 c.e.

A Metaphysical Analysis of the Hebrew Symbols

ALEPH

Aleph א is the first of the Hebrew symbols. Its symbolic number is one. It is one of the three "mothers", and its element is air. Meditatively, it is a major gate of purification, or personal liberation.

Vocally, the letter itself is silent. As it is pronounced with a silent type of breathing, it may be referred to as an aspirate. Its full pronunciation is derived from the fact that it may be spelled out to create a phonetic form using further Hebrew symbols and accompanying vowels. As will be seen with many of the other Hebrew symbols, its metaphysical meaning may be altered or enhanced depending upon the concomitant vowels or spellings that are employed.

When Aleph is spelled out: אָלֶף (aleph lahmed pé) the following meanings may be derived;

1. A Family: denoting the sense of a tribe, which forms a Circle, or something that is enclosed. This may further convey the idea of the womb, and particularly, the fruit of the womb.

2. Oxen: from the idea of yoking or taming, and

therefore bondage. As oxen might be yoked together, a further concept of duality is invoked, along with the implications of polarity and single-ness.

3. A Thousand: which to the ancients contained the meaning of infinite and perpetual. Themes that recur as natural events on a constant basis over an infinite period of time are called the Laws of Truth. Infinite time is in the context of Cosmic Time. Cosmic time is considered to be infinite, since it does not exist in the subjective sense.

When the three Hebrew symbols which make up Aleph א are spelled out with the following vowels: אֶלֶף (aleph lahmed pé) a further set of meanings are created.

1. To Teach: in the process of teaching, or of being taught, comes the force of opening the mind, awareness, insight and enlightenment, in varying degrees.

2. To Utter: which requires the use of breath or air, and denotes a vocal activity. Breath or air has a connection to finite existence, or what is mystical-ly called the "essence". It is what the Greeks called "pneuma", and the Buddhists and Hindus call "prana".

3. To Bring Forth Thousands: conveying a theme of discovery or disclosure; the kind of events that occur suddenly, like a lightening flash. These flashes of wisdom, understanding and insight usu-ally arrive with great clarity if one has the ability to recognize, and even more auspiciously, utilize them in the opening of one's conscious and sub-conscious minds.

Each of the Hebrew symbols has significance in both the physical and metaphysical planes. If one were able to use a measuring cup, the spiritual or metaphysical aspect of Aleph א would far outweigh the physical, as it barely touches the material world. Because of its high level of abstract meaning, Aleph א is often said to be unknowable.

Concepts of the infinite and perpetual are philosophical concepts that are not tangible, but may be expressed in metaphors and allegories that in some measure convey their essence. This is the same language used by musicians and poets, who may, for a time, express the texture of an abstract concept like "love", but not create a material referent to be subjectively examined.

The language of the metaphysical, or spiritual, is the realm of metaphors and allegories. For the moment we may say that a significant portion of Aleph א can only be touched in that infinite world that we shall call the Creator's infinite creation.

Let us return to the denotation of Aleph א as a circle, and expand upon its myriad of meanings. Wheels are circles, spheres such as balls are circular, as is the circumference of the earth. The earth "circles" the sun, while the solar system travels in a circular spiral. The formless, gaseous nebulae rotate in a circular motion. The earliest villages and cities were built in circular configurations, with or without circular walls encompassing them.

The circle is the physical representation of the metaphysical form of spiritual eternity. It represents the perpetual sum of all that is in the universes. A circle (physical or metaphysical) has no beginning and no end. When we talk about a "family circle" on a mundane level, we also imply our genetic heritage or lineage.

The circles of Aleph א are also found in nature in the life/death continuum that perpetually unfolds and dissolves in the Creator's micro/macro universes.

The theme of "bringing forth thousands" indicates that, as the mind opens (particularly on the right, or intuitive, side of the brain) the veils that enfold our subconscious mind commence to fade away. The vast number of perpetual Laws of Truth begin to become evident, and consequently unfold.

"Bringing forth thousands", in Hebrew Scriptures, denotes the innumerable insights that apparently come out of nowhere, those that reach us from the unknowable.

Aleph א is also the first letter in the three spellings for the Hebrew word "God":

EL	אֵל	aleph lahmed
EL-O-HA	אֱלֹהַ	aleph lahmed hé
EL-O-HIM	אֱלֹהִים	aleph lahmed hé yod mem

The Hebrew word commonly called "Lord" in English and spelled יהוה (yod hé vav hé) in Hebrew cannot be pronounced in Hebrew or in any other language. Often referred to as the tetragramaton, the Hebrew word "Adonay" אֲדֹנָי is pronounced instead. This confusion is a result of false knowledge, when the word Lord is incorrectly used in the same context as the word God. The two words are not interchangeable.

Aleph א has a geometric representation, which is a simple dot. And yet the simplest dot is the cornerstone of every other geometric or physical construct.

The dot is a representation of a "monad", which in mystic teaching signifies "one which contains one". However, this "oneness" may be taken a step farther and be compared to an atom, which is a shell that contains a pair of opposites (electrons and protons). Because of this contained duality, it is one of the symbols of the concept of "one which contains two".

In its geometric form, Aleph א signifies the physical representation of the eternal presence of absolute being. In a spiritual sense it is elusive, mysterious and blurred from our senses. It denotes the circle of spiritual eternity, as well as the cosmic point where the spiritual and material come into being. It is also the vanishing point where the visible and invisible part company.

Aleph א represents and functions on the plain of consciousness of the "one which contains one", yet it also partially resides in the realm of "one which contains two". And this is the significance inherent in the "fruit of the womb" outlined earlier.

The Book of Creation, (*Sepher Yetzirah*[4])(III:3), states that "He enthroned the Hebrew symbol Aleph א in air". While some English translations use the word "spirit" for "air", the Hebrew

word that is used in the Sepher Yetzirah is "Shomayim" שָׁמַיִם
shin mem yod mem) which is "air" or "heavens", and *not spirit*.
The common Hebrew word for spirit is "Ruach" רוּחַ (resh vav
het) as in GEN I:2, "and the *spirit* of God hovered over the face of
the waters".

The Hebrew word "air" or "heavens" contains mystical
themes. It is without form, but transports life giving substances.
Light cast through it creates colour. Most of us think of air in
terms of its role as the carrier of life-giving oxygen. In a metaphysical sense, the abstract theme of "emptiness" or "the void"
arises.

Air bridges the finite with the infinite, and the infinite with
the finite.

בּ ב

BETH/VETH   Beth בב is the second Hebrew symbol, and
the first of the seven "doubles". Its symbolic
number is two.

When Beth ב contains a dot in its centre, it is vocalized with
a "b", and pronounced like the English word "bait". Conversely,
without the centre dot ב it is vocalized with a "v" at the beginning.

The symbol alone ב means in, among, near, or before. It
also denotes to or in a place: when one is in a place, there may be
motion or motionlessness.

Beth ב is spelled out as follows: בּית (beth yod tav)

When the vowels are placed in this way; בִּית (beth yod
tav), Beth ב has the significance of to tame, or domesticate.

When the vowels are placed in the following way; בַּית
(bayt yod tav) it means house or home. Other metaphysical
meanings are lineage, heredity, origin, or source. As it is also a
receptacle, it brings things to rest. We may also say that what has
been brought to rest has been stabilized. Metaphysically, Beth ב
signifies *without motion*. We should consider it to be stationary.

While the geometric configuration for Aleph א was a dot, Beth ב goes one step further: in terms of the universe, it is like two nebulae that are separated from each other, but may be connected by a *line*. One might also think of them as two connected molecules, for instance, salt.

The Book of Creation states that, "He enthroned Beth ב in Life". Metaphysically, life has a relationship with the soul and spirit. It is also linked to the vital source of breath. Further, life encompasses physical existence: it has substance, or form. Nature comprises the world of life.

As previously stated, בִּיתֿ (beth yod tav) means a house or receptacle. It is the metaphysical archetype of all dwellings. The container (and its contents) are stationary – just *there*. The vessel is a support for its contents, which cannot stand alone.

As a double symbol, Beth expresses the coming into being of our spiritual and physical existences, which both occupy a single receptacle or container.

The Hebrew symbols Aleph, Beth אב express all that comes into existence spiritually from the source of an ongoing Creation. In the five Books of Moses, the *Torah*, the first two words (GEN 1:1) start with the symbol Beth ב: "In the beginning" *"B're'shiyth b'ara"* בְּרָא בְּרֵאשִׁית (beth resh aleph shin yod tav beth resh aleph). The third word, "Elohim" commences with the symbol Aleph א: אֱלֹהִים (aleph lahmed hé yod final mem)— "God".

A more detailed explanation of why the Hebrew Scriptures commence with the second letter of the Hebrew symbols is the subject of the chapter entitled, *In the Beginning*.

גג
GIMMEL

Gimmel גג is the third Hebrew symbol, and the second of the seven "doubles". Its symbolic number is three. When Gimmel ג contains a dot in its centre it is vocalized with a hard "g", as in "get". Without the dot ג it is pronounced with a soft "g", as in "geometry". Gimmel גֿ alone has no Hebrew meaning, however when it is spelled out with the following vowels גָמַל (gimmel mem lahmed) it means to ripen, wean, or mature. It may also have the connotation to reward or remunerate.

When the following vowels are utilized, גָּמָל (gimmel mem lahmed) it means camel. If these vowels are used, גַּמֵל (gimmel mem lahmed) the meaning is to drive a camel. To wean, ripen or mature ranges in metaphysical thought through the evolution of all animals, minerals, and plants, including, of course, human evolution.

The camel was often typified as a creature of forbearance and patience, as well as possessing its renowned capacity for carrying water. It is capable of completing long journeys while enduring suffering (as in the context of a burden bearer or in labouring).

Human parallels may easily be associated with this image. The "motion" implied in driving a camel takes Gimmel גֿ one step further than the motionlessness of the symbol Beth בֿ. Something new is evolving.

Gimmel is a *female* principle (see Chapter I) which represents life's pulsation (motion) in every living part of every living organism. The symbol bears witness to the throb of divinity that exists in all things. The female principle is a life-maturing and preserving reservoir.

The harmonious union that evolves from Beth- Aleph (בא) - "In the beginning, God created..." — commences to evolve through Gimmel גֿ. Beth בֿ is in Aleph א as Aleph א is in Beth בֿ, evolving through Gimmel גֿ. The geometric representation of Gimmel גֿ is the triangle, which is the simplest structure that maintains a form.

A two-dimensional figure (ie. having only width and length) is not sufficient to geometrically interpret the invariable triangles associated with metaphysics, as three dimensions are required. The three-dimensional triangle contains ten entities that make up its form, and twenty-two to complete its abstract form. Details on the geometric aspects of the Hebrew symbols will be presented in the section dealing with geometry.

The Book of Creation states that "He enthroned Gimmel ‏ג‏
in well-being" (or wealth). The state of well-being in the metaphysical sense is synonymous with happiness, euphoria and bliss.
However there is a further connotation of quiet, peace and con-
tentment. Health and sustenance are metaphysical abstractions of
wealth.

The awesome theme of a deep reverence for Life flows
through the history of Qabbal teaching: indeed throughout the
framework of Hebrew culture itself. The very essence of love and
compassion which emanates from a single, imageless Creator is
embodied in Aleph Beth Gimmel ‏אבג‏.

The scriptural significance of honoring one's mother and
father infers that one should reflect upon one's lineage in a unique
and sacred way. The emphasis in EX XX:12, "Not to kill" may be
viewed in the same manner, and unselectively extended to all living things.

One might further consider the implications of GEN IX:4,
"only flesh with the life thereof, which is the blood thereof, shall
ye not eat", which is the foundation of the Jewish dietary law of
"Kashrut" or Kosher. Kashrut is derived from the Hebrew
"Kadosh" ‏קָדוֹשׁ‏ – Holy.

‏דּ‏

DALETH

Daleth ‏דד‏ is the fourth of the Hebrew symbols, and the third of the seven "doubles". It
is pronounced "da-leth". Its symbolic number
is four. Daleth ‏ד‏ alone has no Hebrew meaning. The symbol is
comprised of the following Hebrew symbols, ‏דלת‏ (daleth
lahmed tav) and has no meaning until the following vowels are
placed in this way, ‏דֶּלֶת‏ (daleth lahmed tav). At this point
Daleth ‏ד‏ denotes an entrance, gate, door, or portal, which may
further be taken to infer a passageway or corridor. While a door
may be both an access point or a barrier, Daleth ‏ד‏ may be metaphysically thought of as a direct approach through a passage. And

yet the passageway may be obstructed. In the plural form דְּלָתַיִם (D'la tayim), the word means dual, as in double doors, or a two-leaved gate. Double doors or gates are known metaphysically as "Gates of Illumination", and contain the significance of the uterus, womb, birth canal and vagina. One who passes through the Gates of Illumination has passed through a transition of consciousness.

Daleth ד is the emergence into the here and now – physical existence. The geometry of Daleth ד in a two-dimensional mode is the square. In a three-dimensional configuration, it is a cube. Both the square and the cube are the metaphysical symbols of material knowledge. They are perceived to be stable and permanent.

The Book of Creation states that "He enthroned Daleth ד in Wisdom", which encompasses mental processes, concentration, caution, knowledge of the abstract, and the ability to enlarge the mind. This is a poignant way of expressing the state of mind which belongs to one who has passed through the Gates of Illumination.

As previously stated, Daleth ד is representative of the number four. Nearly all spellings of the sacred word, Lord, in spiritual worship have four letters:

Yod Hé Vav Hé	יהוה Hebrew
Lord	English
Dieu	French
Gott	German
Odin	Norse (Scandinavian)
Jove	Roman
Zeus	Greek
Atma	Hindu
Nebo	Assyrian
Isis	Egyptian

ה

HE

Hé ה is the fifth Hebrew symbol, and the first of the twelve "singles". It is pronounced like the English word "hay". Its symbolic number is five.

The singular symbol ה placed before a Hebrew word means "the", as in "the valley". When it appears at the end of a place name, it becomes a directional article, as in "to Jerusalem".

When Hé ה appears alone, or in its full spelling, הֵא (hé aleph) with vowels in place, the meaning is as expressed above. However, some confusion may set in when the two-symbol form is used to delineate, "Lo!" or "Behold!", or a question mark.

The metaphysical significance of this symbol could fill a book of its own. The articles "the" and "to" are common grammar, and have no special metaphysical meaning. However, when the emphasized words "Lo!" and "Behold!" הֵן appear, as in GEN XLVII:23; DAN III:25; EZ XVI:43, there is an entirely new depth of meaning – to see!

When one sees, one is said to have sight, and herein lies the key to the unravelling of Hé ה.

If one is to see correctly, one must train oneself to become the observer, and not the observed. The difference might be likened to the interaction in a team sports activity: the spectator (observer) sees the overview of the entire game, whereas the participant (observed) sees only his/her own perspective of what is happening in the limited area around him/herself. The participant has limited sight, and only sees a portion of the "Truth" of the game. And yet if the observer sees the game through the eyes of another, i.e. on television, only a part of the overview is glimpsed. The observer's point of view would be further diminished if the news of the game were to be gleaned through reading or hearing about the event. In these instances, the observer only receives partial truth.

The symbol Hé ה emphasizes that one must be the *direct*

observer, or discoverer in order to "see" the whole truth. In Hebrew Qabbal teaching, these acts of discovery are called revelations and insights. These direct revelations and insights lead one to True Knowledge.

There are many phrases that are commonly used to describe this unique acquisition of sight: "I twigged onto it", or "I had my eyes opened" are two. Moreover, there are different levels of seeing, or sight. While one may "twig onto it" now and then, one may also do the same on a constant basis. The former more often than not leads to half-truths, while the latter leads to whole Truths.

If one can utilize one's lifetime to be open and to see clearly, one has the potential to gain enlightened awareness.

The geometric configuration of Hé ה is a combination of those used in Aleph א Beth ב Gimmel ג and Daleth ד plus a circle and a rectangle. It contains in geometric form the essences of Creation in Aleph/Beth אב, and carries through the preceding symbols in the same evolutionary manner. As previously mentioned, the triangle of Gimmel ג is the simplest structure that maintains a form, and the square or cube that is defined in Daleth ד signifies material form. Material form is metaphysically referred to as material or outer knowledge. The circle that is added by Hé ה to this ongoing process represents eternity: perpetuity that has no beginning, and no end. The rectangle personifies knowledge gained that may contain falsehoods, and is then referred to as false knowledge.

The Book of Creation states that, "He enthroned Hé ה in Sight".

The twenty-two Hebrew symbols are founded on the pivotal value of five which, as previously indicated, is the symbolic number of Hé ה.

ו

VAV

Vav ו is the sixth Hebrew symbol, and the second of the twelve "singles". The symbol may be pronounced "vuv" as in "vulnerable". Its symbolic number is six. Vav ו alone means *and, also, but, therefore,* and *then.*

When spelled out, using the appropriate vowels, וָו (vav vav) its metaphysical meaning is a hook or a peg. Vav also acts to turn the past into the future, and the future to the past.

The metaphysical significance of a hook begins with the concept of a device that couples things together, and serves the purpose of an anchor or safeguard. As a hanger, a hook is a support, like a frame. Further, a hook usually has at least one fairly sharp edge, and can be synonymous with a sword, or scythe. A sharp edge deflects, and may send what it deflects into turmoil.

The word "hook" (the symbols וָו vav vav) appears only nine times in the Hebrew Scriptures: EX XXVI; XXVII; XXXVI, and XXXVIII. Significantly, these sections deal with the instructions on how the Temple in the Wilderness is to be constructed.

The geometric configuration for Vav ו is the sum of the preceding five Hebrew symbols, plus an interlocking equilateral triangle, where one triangle points up, the other down. In Hebrew Qabbal teaching, the triangle pointing upwards is coloured red representing male energy (active) while the triangle pointing downwards is coloured blue for female energy (passive). This is one of the Hebrew Qabbal symbols of balanced equilibrium.

The Book of Creation states that "He enthroned Vav ו in Hearing". This adds a further dimension to the metaphysics outlined above: one may listen, but not "hear"!

By hearing, one may become informed, or mindful. This is a form of seeing that was discussed earlier. The act of hearing allows one to delve deeper into a subject, to peek behind the curtain, as it were, and to open one's eyes.

The most poignant use of the word *hear* in the Hebrew

Scriptures occurs in DEUT VI:4: "Hear, O Israel, the Lord our God, the Lord is One".

ZAYIN

Zayin זּ is the seventh Hebrew symbol, and the third of the twelve "singles". It is pronounced to rhyme with wine. Its symbolic number is seven.

Zayin זּ alone has no Hebrew meaning, however its meaning changes depending upon the vowel placements. When it is spelled out in its full form: זַיִן (zayin yod nun) means weapon, while זִיֵן (zayin yod nun) means to arm, as well as *ornament*, or *to adorn*.

As a spiritual metaphor, a weapon is a resource. It is an instrument which requires skill in its use as a deterrent or a defence. As a defence, it is likened to a shield that preserves and acts as a balance of power. As a traditional Biblical weapon, the sword was used both offensively and defensively, which brings to it the significance of a struggle or battle. The raising of one's spiritual consciousness may also be seen as a struggle or a battle: at times one is defensive; at others, one should go at it aggressively. As a sword is sharp-edged, a sharp two-edged sword, in a metaphysical sense, aids one in cutting through to the Truth: the sword "parts the way", so that the approach to the Truth is clearer. Zayin זּ is often referred to as the "sword of Judah".

When Zayin זּ is used in the sense of to arm, it is metaphysically linked to the word weapon. It also evokes the thought that the arm and hand are called into play in order to wield it, as well as being our providers (more so in Biblical times than the present). Arms and hands are one's first line of physical defence. Zayin זּ when used to mean ornament, or to adorn, has the metaphysical significance of making something better. When an object is polished or refined it becomes more beautiful, radiant and brilliant, it glows with the reflection of light.

One's spiritual being is enriched when it is similarly polished or refined, it has the chance to glow. And the more one goes into battle with the appropriate spiritual weapon, the more purified and refined is the result.

The sharp, two-edged sword aids in the approach to Truth. The geometric configuration for Zayin ז adds an inner square and seven inner circles to the pattern that has been evolving through the previous six Hebrew symbols. The seven circles represent the spheres of the Universe.

One should review the geometric symbols that are discussed in Chapter 5, along with their metaphysical meanings, in order to discover the balanced harmony that unfolds through them.

The Book of Creation states "He enthroned Zayin ז in smell". In order to smell something, two things must be called into play: the sense organ represented by one's physical nose, and the inner/outer breath. The breath contains the Spirit, or the essence of the Universe. Whether the result of the act is deemed to be pleasant or unpleasant, there is an implied act of discovery. In the metaphysical sense, discovery brings insight and revelation. No matter how insignificant in terms of quantity, it is still insight and revelation. Inherent in the act of smelling is the fact that it enables us to set things apart, and to discriminate between opposites. This basis for comparison allows one to distinguish, for example, the difference between sour and sweet. Without one to parallel and counterbalance the other, the distinctions would be meaningless. One requires the knowledge of opposites to learn and to grow. It is in a similar way that one's discoveries lead one to defend or to attack, and one uses inner and outer weapons to accomplish this.

As breath is the prime vehicle of smell, it is like a weapon, or a device with which one may ornament oneself. It is a major pathway to Truth.

HET

Het ח is the eighth Hebrew symbol, and the fourth of the twelve "singles". Its symbolic number is eight. Het may be vocalized in two ways: the first is as it appears; the second, as if the "H" were a gargled "CHHH".

The symbol alone has no Hebrew meaning. You will notice that there are two depictions of Het above. The first, ח, is used in common print, and the other, ‎יִי‎, is used in the hand-made Torahs (the five books of Moses) that rest in the Sanctuary Arks in Synagogues. This sacred form of the symbol, meaning "Lo!" and "Behold!" may also be found in some Orthodox Jewish prayer books, and is taught in some Orthodox Jewish schools.

This is not a closely guarded secret, yet only those who have read from the Synagogue scrolls, practised orthodox prayer, or attended a school where it is taught would be aware of this form of Het. And of those who have, very few would be aware of the Hebrew Qabbal connection.

However, it is this uncommon form of Het that is the key to the metaphysical understanding of the symbol. Two Zayins ‎יִי‎ facing forward, with a triangular-shaped sign above and joining them create the symbol. First, we will discuss Het ח spelled out, and then the double Zayin, ‎יִי‎, form of the symbol.

חט (het teth) with the accompanying vowels means canine tooth, incisor tooth, chisel, and plough bit.

A canine is a domesticated dog (or animal, in this case), which in the metaphorical sense is a living being who has been tamed and domesticated, but still has deeply rooted animal tendencies.

A tooth infers an object which has a cutting edge, but while it is sharp, it does not cut cleanly. Teeth are also a metaphor for a fortification or defence. The teeth are a first line of defence for what exits the open mouth, and the second line of fortification for what enters.

A plough bit parts the earth, one does one's planting, and then places earth over what has been planted. Nature then takes over and brings forth what has been planted in its truthful form. The seed that has been planted, while bearing no physical resemblance to the finished growth, contains all the potential material to bring it to fruition, or to its final form.

A chisel has a sharp cutting edge. Used correctly, it creates form and shape, and can be used for very rough or extremely refined work. As a tool or instrument, it can shape the most precious gems or the largest blocks of stone.

The uncommon composition of Het חֿ, is similar to that for Zayin, with two exceptions. The first deals with the concept that there are two Zayins זֿז that are identical twins, or doubles. The other deals with the triangular form above the Zayins חֿ. Metaphysically, two infers duality and polarity. Doubles have a unity that is both inner and outer. This mirrors one's outer form and one's inner being.

The triangular form above the two Zayins חֿ is a pyramid, which is the geometric symbol of Het ח. The upward pointing pyramid of Het חֿ represents the earth's Northern Hemisphere. The proportions of the pyramid have a direct relationship with the dimensions of the earth, and the earth's distance from the sun. These measurements can be determined without the use of mathematics. The pyramid evolves on its own with the unfolding of the Hebrew Qabbal geometry.

The symbol is like a balanced gate that beckons one to pass through.

The Book of Creation states that "He enthroned Het ח in Speech". Speech, in other words, is language, the voice and sound. The dangers of improper speech were known to the ancient Hebrew Sages. They set this teaching down in the Tower of Babel story, GEN XI:1-9.

Speech is the effect of one pattern interacting with another. It may embody the wickedest sword of all. It is mainly used as a trading weapon, "What do you need, and what can we trade?"

Speech is also used mainly in a selfish sense, for the sake of ourselves. It is one of the main sources of negative action/reaction. These negative actions/reactions keep our consciousness in a state of confusion, a Tower of Babel state. The almost constant intellectual chatter (or babble) that takes place in one's unfocussed mind is a barrier to clear, concentrated awareness. In order to pass through the gate of Het ח, one must learn to put one's inner and outer speech in harmonious balance. The clear comprehension of the speech of *silence* is required in order to lead one to the key to this gate.

ט

TETH   Teth ט is the ninth Hebrew symbol and the fifth of the twelve "singles". It is pronounced like the word "tame", with the "me" at the end being replaced with a "t". Its symbolic number is nine.

Teth ט alone has no Hebrew meaning, however when it is spelled out טיט (teth yod teth) it means mire and/or clay. This meaning may be extended to encompass a swamp or quagmire into which one may fall or go over the edge in the spiritual sense: one may be overwhelmed or engulfed as a result of not being on "solid ground".

The process of spiritual evolution can be fraught with swamp-like traps that are much like clay: pliable, and more often than not leading to a state of euphoria. These are walls or obstacles that may lead one away from the "green pastures" alluded to in Scriptures. PSALMS XL and LXIX, as well as JOB XL are excellent examples of the metaphysics of this symbol.

Teth's ט symbolic number is the metaphysical number of the completion of a specific cycle. The geometric configuration of Teth ט combines the total of the previous eight Hebrew symbols (completing the geometric cycle), and depicts the ten Sephiroth (singular "Sephira"), the main Hebrew Qabbal "energy centres". The Sephiroth, areas of study and practice unto themselves, which cannot be seen by the physical senses; however, they can be experienced through meditation. They are vehicles or vessels through which spiritual transformation or purification may take place. Sephiroth are not static like their geometric counterparts, but have individual rates of pulsation and their own cycles. The wheels of conventional watch movements which move back and forth provide a good illustration of their motion.

In most humans, the Sephiroth are "blocked". Meditation practice works to clear these energy centres so that the luminous light of eternity may be freed. When the centres are opened and clear, they become a major factor in raising one's state of spiritual awareness.

It is advisable to do this practice with the guidance of an experienced meditation teacher. The ancient Hebrew Sages referred to the connotations of this symbol as a mire/swamp for rather sagacious reasons, and it is not to be taken lightly.

The Book of Creation states that "He enthroned Teth ט in eating". The physical act of eating commences with the use of the mouth. Metaphysically, the mouth is a gate or passageway. In this respect, Teth ט has a direct relationship with Het ח.

The act of eating has three main divisions. The first is the activity of inhaling, or taking within us the life-giving essence of Creation. The second deals with awareness, specifically the awareness of the purity of what one is absorbing. The third concerns detecting the effect of what one has consumed upon one's physical and spiritual bodies. Since, like a mire or swamp, Teth ט implies a trap, eating may be put to the wrong use, or wasted. It may also give one pain or prolonged agony. Like being trapped in a mire, without clear awareness, we may eat without discrimination or discernment. One may feed one's physical senses to the point of euphoria, which leads to artificial highs and lows, leaving one in the middle of a swamp with feet of clay.

י

YOD

Yod י is the tenth Hebrew symbol and the sixth of the twelve "singles". The "y" and the "d" have the standard pronunciations found in English, however the "o" in the centre may be pronounced either as a hard "o", or as a soft "u". Its symbolic number is ten.

Yod י alone has no Hebrew meaning, however it has two spellings: the contemporary יוד (yod vav daleth) and the Biblical יָד (yod daleth). The writer has not been able to accurately determine when nor why the change in spelling took place. In the metaphysical interpretation which follows, however, there is still a close link between both spellings.

יוד (yod vav daleth) in contemporary usage means iodine, in the sense of an inhibitor or preventive. Iodine is also a cleanser. As an inhibitor, it acts as a safety valve; as a cleanser, it has the sense of clearing away.

It is also the root for the Hebrew word "knowing" and of the Greek *Gnostic,* one who knows, and therefore has wisdom and understanding.

יָד (yod daleth) means "a hand" (an open one), indicating natural energy, power and direction. A hand is at the outer edge and is used to sense. To hand something on is to connect or to cross over. In this sense it has the power to propagate. A hand is also an indicator or pointer; it is like a signal lamp giving direction.

The Book of Creation states that "He enthroned Yod י in coition". This is *not* the hidden explanation for sexual intercourse; metaphysically, it has the sense of the intimacy of consumating a union on a spiritual level of consciousness. This union or pairing creates a spontaneous flowering, which in turn has power and direction. The act of "flowering" also contains the essence of fertility and maturation, not in years, but in terms of mind consciousness.

KAF

Kaf כ‍ך is the eleventh Hebrew symbol, and the fourth of the seven "doubles". It is pronounced with a hard "k", soft "a", and an "f". Its symbolic number is twenty.

The symbol כ alone signifies a comparison, as in the English words as, like, when, at, about, according to. With different vowels כ‍ף (kaf pé) the symbol means before. It can be found in the Hebrew Scriptures before the words Lord, and God. When used as a comparison it could read – "as" white as light.

When spelled out כ‍ף (kaf pé) it means the hollow or palm of the hand. It also means the sole of the foot, or the bowl-shaped portion of a vessel. The word has the sense of being a receptacle. Power is associated with Kaf כ, similar to the tenth symbol, Yod י. The power is reflected in the adage, "I have them in the palm of my hand". Moreover, this statement creates both positive and negative emotional reactions, a traditional Hebrew Qabbal duality.

In the context of a receptacle, the metaphysics of Kaf כ reflect nourishment or a lack thereof. In the positive sense, it contains the nourishment of something that strengthens, sustains and stabilizes. A receptacle may have the depth of an abyss, which may be deep enough to be a void. A void eliminates, displaces and cleanses. The end result is purification, a form of transformation. In the opposite or negative perspective, a cup may contain afflictions. In Hebrew Scriptures, these are represented as plagues, adversity, poverty, and pain.

Kaf כ is the first letter of the Hebrew word *K'li* כ‍ל‍י for both receptacle or vessel. This is not merely coincidental; Noah's Ark and the Tabernacle each contain the significance of a vessel as does the statement "my cup runneth over" in PSALM 23.

In Christian teaching, a chalice or goblet is used to encompass the same metaphysical principles.

The Book of Creation states that "He enthroned Kaf כ in wealth". Spiritual wealth is typified by the land flowing with milk and honey. It is a state of euphoric well-being, obtained through love, compassion, wisdom and understanding. It is the metaphysical wealth of limitless resources. In Hebrew Scriptures wealth is exemplified by Solomon's riches.

Implicit in the symbol Kaf כ is cause and effect, action and reaction, which evokes the Hebrew word *mazal* מַזָּל. Mazal, meaning *constellation*, reflects the actions and effects of cosmic and universal energies. In the Far East it is called "karma". Kaf כ contains the concept of the intuitive discovery that the earth and its contents are a reflection or shadow of the cosmic purpose. Each of us can become an open reservoir of the ways and means to spiritual freedom. One can open this reservoir and hold it in the palm of one's hand, becoming a storehouse of resources as limitless as the riches of Solomon. It can then be said that one has inherited the land flowing with milk and honey.

ל

LAHMED   Lahmed ל is the twelfth Hebrew symbol, and the seventh of the twelve "singles". It is pronounced "lah-med". Its symbolic number is thirty.

Grammatically, Lahmed ל translates as *unto, into, towards, during, to, for, about, according to,* or *belonging to.*

When Lammed is spelled out with these vowels לָמֶד (lahmed mem daleth) it means *to teach, to goad, accustom to,* and infers a belonging to the source. Lahmed ל also means to learn. Learning and teaching are opposites, thus the word has a pairing.

It might seem that learning and teaching are actions in opposition, however a Teacher either knows or does not know, or a student is either learning or is not learning. Lahmed ל represents the true act of spiritual progression. It signifies, on the one hand, the open capacity to learn, and on the other hand, the great adventure of self-discovery and self-direction. In this sense, the two acts are paired.

A large degree of quiet-minded awareness is required to

teach what has been learned, and one discovers and learns from teaching. The depth of Hebrew Qabbal teaching is such that this pairing process is continuously ongoing, as stated in JOB XXI:22, "shall any teach God knowledge".

The Book of Creation states that "He enthroned Lahmed ל in work" – a strange word for a spiritual or metaphysical teaching! However, at this point in *this work* it should be rather self-evident that the raising of the spiritual consciousness does not happen by itself. In fact, a great deal of practice and continuous use are required.

This work eventually brings forth the prodigious capacities of a truly free will that learning and teaching produces. The rewards of this work are an active stimulated energy accompanied by eyes that "see" and ears that "hear".

מ
MEM   Mem מ is the thirteenth Hebrew symbol, and the second of the three "Mothers". The transliteral spelling is usually accepted as "Mem". Its symbolic number is forty.

Mem מ alone has no Hebrew meaning. However when the three symbols that comprise it are spelled out with these vowels מַיִם (mem yod mem) it means water. The words water, spring, and other similarly associated words are the only ones attached to this symbol.

Metaphysically, water is the metaphor of the reflection of our unseeable consciousness – all aspects of the mind. If the water is turbulent or muddy, one's mind reflects the same condition. When one's mind is in a state of turmoil, what one senses is also in this unwholesome condition. The problem is that what one sees through this unclear water is perceived as reality. However, it is only when the water is clear and calm that one actually experiences true reality.

The world that one assumes that one sees, and one's perception of oneself, are actually *illusions*. This is metaphysically referred to as the "suspended mind".

The Hebrew symbol Mem מ is a major gate of purification and transformation.

The Book of Creation states that "He enthroned Mem מ in water". The explanation is the same as that stated above.

נ
NUN

Nun נ is the fourteenth Hebrew symbol, and the eighth of the twelve "singles". The simplest transliteration is the English word "noon". Some dialects pronounce the central "u" as a soft "u". This writer prefers the latter pronunciation.

The symbolic number of Nun נ is fifty.

Nun נ alone has no Hebrew meaning. When it is spelled out נון (nun vav nun) it means *be continued, to be perpetual, to resprout.*

Some Western teachings define Nun נון (nun vav nun) as "fish", This is an Aramaic meaning which does not appear in Hebrew Scriptures. In order to remain consistent and not read into the metaphysics something that is not there, we will stay within the Hebrew Scripture meanings.

The word "continue" has a powerful metaphysical base. Its foundation is the verb "to be". This is the same root from whence "I am that I am" (EX III:14) sprouts.

The metaphysical meaning of "continue" refers to the sheer delight of existing. It is living and existing in the complete circle and depth of the word — past, present and future. Solomon is spoken of in PSALMS 72:17 as follows: "May his name be continued as long as the sun". Likened to an incomprehensible length of time into the future, it completes the sphere and pops up in pre-existence. Perpetuity speaks of something that has continuous existence. There is a sense of being alive and of also being indestructable or immortal. This evokes themes of existence and nonexistence, mortality and immortality, and impermanence.

Mem מ the symbol of the radiant crystal clear mind is appropriately followed by "impermanence", which illustrates that this insight is required in order for one to comprehend perpetuity, mortality/immortality, and thereby lose the fear of the death/life cycles.

The immortality of the soul is a fundamental principle in Gnostic Hebrew Qabbal teaching. Physical existence ends when one's "mission" or purpose in that particular lifetime has been completed: it is time to move on. Death is merely a stage in the evolution of the soul. One unidentified Hebrew Qabbal master stated that "Death is merely moving from one home to another. If we are wise, we will make the latter the more beautiful home."

Something that is perpetual or continuous cannot be nailed down; it is ever-changing, without a fixed state or form. To take the concept a step further, a "thing" has substance, while "nothing" is devoid of substance. That which has no substance is not permanent. In other words, it is impermanent. Further extensions of impermanence yield a theme of formlessness that cannot be described in any conventional sense.

To the intellectual mind, this type of "non-form" corresponds to the abstract notion of "nothing". Nothing implies no-*thing* – it is neuter, without opposites (since they do not exist) – it has dissolved.

Part of the process of spiritual awakening is the dissolution of the opposites within the individual being. Impermanence embodies change, and lacks uniformity. It may move from form to vapour in much the same way that water may be transformed from a fluid to steam and back again.

In terms of human existence, perpetuity is analogous to the concepts of mortality and immortality – the life/death, death/life continuum, or cycle. The Book of Creation states that "He enthroned Nun נ in walking".

When one walks, one may follow, be beside, or be in front. This forms a metaphysical trilogy. One may also move slowly or quickly, again a set of opposites. If the walk is aimless, it is similar to a scattered mind leading nowhere. If the walk follows a trail, it has direction and leads somewhere.

Another aspect of walking is being in a procession. There is the sense of something preceding and following: once more, a continuum on a path.

ס

SAMEKH   Samekh ס is the fifteenth Hebrew symbol, and the ninth of the twelve "singles". The transliteration into English is "saw-mak", with a soft "a". Its symbolic number is sixty.

The symbol Samekh ס alone has no Hebrew meaning. When it is spelled out it has the following vowels, סָמֶךְ (samekh mem kaf) but no meaning. Samekh ס is one of the more difficult Hebrew symbols to comprehend, as the product of this symbol is more abstract. When the following vowels are added to the symbol spelled out, סָמֶךְ (samekh mem kaf) it can mean *to lean upon, to trust in, to stand fast, to sustain, a reference point,* and *a fulcrum.*

Metaphysically, it is the awareness of the gift or legacy of the spiritual or mystic communion with the Creator. Intuitive understanding does not mean blind trust, however. It is through the discovery of causes and effects that one gleans an awareness. It is as though there has been a clear unfolded revelation that can sustain and strengthen the one who has made the discovery. This act of disclosure is like a scale which can maintain perfect balance and equilibrium.

One's consciousness can still contain hope and fear, joy and anxiety, but because there is some control over the balancing point, or fulcrum, there is the knowledge that all is coming together; the rays of hope that flickered on and off are now singular. Once a foothold is secure, a refreshing surge of courage and clear perception arise.

The Book of Creation states that "He enthroned Samekh ס

in anger". To most of us, anger is an absolute negative of excitable
fire and fury. On the positive side, however, anger stirs the fires of
energy – it goads us on. This form of excitement sets off energy
vibrations that can produce manifestations of discovery. If the fire
and fury are accomplished with clear awareness, the aftermath is
sustained clarity and strength for the discoverer.

עֹ

A'YIN   A'yin עֹ is the sixteenth Hebrew symbol, and
                  the tenth of the twelve "singles". It is pro-
nounced as the English word "wine", without the "w". The closest
pronunciation would be "eye-yin", without a pause. Its symbolic
number is seventy.

A'yin עֹ alone has no Hebrew meaning. When it is spelled
out with the following vowels, עַיִן (a'yin yod nun), it has a wide
range of meanings. The most important ones in the metaphysical
sense are eye, sight, appearance, conceit, humble, knowledge, and
fountain (as in the eye of the landscape).

The eye is an organ of vision that, unaided, perceives light.
But as an organ of sight, its vision is limited, so what it sees physically keeps one in ignorance of the greater whole. On a purely
physical level, its function cannot render the entire picture, therefore one's knowledge is actually false. Most people rely on this
false knowledge for their inner and outer daily activities.

Metaphysically, the eye and sight blend together. When one
"sets one's sights" one concentrates. Through trained concentration one can achieve clear, unaided mental sight. This clarity of
vision exposes the limited perception one experiences in the purely physical sense. One comes nearer the Truth. Appearances are,
in fact, deceiving. One can control whether one is looking *on* or
looking *in*. If one relies on false knowledge, one fools oneself. The
end result is often a large dose of ego or conceit.

The Hebrew Qabbal on the metaphysical plane considers
the eye as a symbol of clear mental sight, light, or spiritual per-

ception. This form of metaphysical perception is the eternal root of all boundless existence. It enables one to distinguish illusion from Truth.

The Book of Psalms (CXV:4,5) states that those who worship idols have eyes but cannot see.

> "Their idols are silver and gold,
>
> The work of men's hands.
>
> They have mouths, but they speak not.
>
> Eyes have they, but they see not."

The Book of Creation states that "He enthroned A'yin ע in mirth" – the absurd, bizarre and seemingly senseless – very often "black humour". If one considers what may be found to be metaphysically "funny", it is the senseless suffering that is created by the absurdities and fanciful ignorance of those without clear sight. One may indeed be the author of one's own misfortunes.

PÉ

Pé פפ is the seventeenth Hebrew symbol, and the fifth of the seven "doubles". When a dot occurs in the centre of the symbol, the pronunciation is "pay" or "peh". Without the dot, the pronunciation is "fay" or "feh". The traditionally used sound is "pay" or "fay". Its symbolic number is eighty.

Pé פ alone has no Hebrew meaning, however there are two methods of spelling the symbol. Both are accurate, as they come from the same ancient root. The first is פא (pé aleph). The second is פה (pé hé). Both spellings can be found as two separate words in JOB XXXVIII:11.

To add to the confusion, a change of vowels can also change the meaning, but the purpose of this work is to discuss the metaphysical base, rather than intellectualize over grammar.

The first example above with the accompanying vowels פא (pé aleph) has the ancient root meaning of a demonstrative force.

The second spelling with its vowels פֶּה (pé hé) also has the same ancient root and means "of a demonstrative force". The commonly accepted metaphysical spelling with these accompanying vowels is פֵּה (pé hé).

All three are correct for metaphysical meanings. Their combinations and sounds for meditation purposes change depending upon the function intended by the meditation teacher. To investigate the meaning "of a demonstrative force", one must first contemplate that something demonstrative is natural, harmonious, deep-rooted, loving, or affectionate. The end result is an offering of meaningful evidence that what is felt affects the senses. It is positive and friendly if it is truly demonstrative. A force has strength that one may associate with sufficient amplitude, or even a violence that is capable of demolishing obstructions. Imagine that what stands in its way is forced or blown open. This force or strength is not linear; it has the dimension of the cosmic universe. It is awesome. Such a demonstrative force would leave those affected with a knowledge of indescribable warmth, leavening and maturing of mind.

פֵּה (pé hé) with these accompanying vowels means mouth, speech, command, border, or edge. In the context of mouth or speech it is meant as a means of blowing. One's speech/mouth is often the vehicle for a negative demonstrative force.

The Book of Creation states that "He enthroned Pé פ in beauty". Beauty implies a masterpiece – a final result of perfect, balanced harmony. Nature, and the cosmic universe are examples of the perfection of the brilliant, radiant light that emanates from Creation, a process that has been ongoing for unimaginable eons. Like the miracle of breathing, it is painless, peaceful, blissful, and divine.

צ

TZADI   Tzadi צ is the eighteenth Hebrew symbol and the eleventh of the twelve "singles". The "Tz" should be slurred together as "ts". The "a" is pronounced "ah", and the "di" as "dee". Phonetically, it would be written "tsahdee". Its symbolic number is ninety.

Tzadi צ alone has no Hebrew meaning. When the symbol itself is spelled out it has these vowels צָדִי (tzadi daleth yod). When the symbol is spelled out with these vowels צַדִי (tzadi daleth yod) it means side, or lateral.

The common Biblical pronunciation of the symbol as found in EX XXVI:13 is צַדֵי (tzadi daleth yod) is a plural.

Metaphysically, a side, or sides, encompass only a part of the whole. They are also the edge or extremities of a main body. This movement from the lateral implies motion. As an abstract activity, something may move laterally in more than one direction at a time. In Metaphysics, this motion is referred to as being from East to West, or from West to East. This is an esoteric way of saying from inner to outer, or from outer to inner.

The choosing of sides comes from a free will that is capable of exercising discretion and judgment. Does one go with the material world or the spiritual? Does one try to move up a balanced middle path? In the world of the Hebrew Qabbal, this can be truly determined from the flashes and ongoing manifestations of self-discovery and insight. The stage is set for the choice of coming into being, or of passing away.

Pride, vanity and ostentation may be smoothed over sufficiently to allow love, compassion, wisdom and understanding in their complete manifestations to come forth.

The Book of Creation states that "He enthroned Tzadi צ in thought". Thought is an imageless mental process. For the majority of humanity, it is a concert of wandering thoughts, usually swift and instantaneous. Thoughts may come with the speed of lightning, or have the shock effect of one's being hit by lightning. Throughout this process the intellect makes ongoing judgments. Often there is an indescriminate changing of sides.

The thoughts settle in the choosing of one side – for those who have the eyes that see and the ears that hear.

ק
QOF

Qof ק is the nineteenth Hebrew symbol, and the twelfth of the twelve "singles". Phonetically, it would be pronounced to rhyme with "hoof". Its symbolic number is one hundred.

Qof ק alone has no metaphysical meaning, however it has two distinct meanings when different vowel placements are used in its full spelling. קוף (qof vav pé) with the accompanying vowels means ape or monkey. קוף (qof vav pé) with these accompanying vowels means "eye of a needle", or the hole in an axe head. Both vowel placements spell out the symbol correctly and both meanings lead to the same metaphysical discovery or understanding.

In the negative sense, a monkey is an imitator or copy-cat. It has always been depicted as a flatterer in its ability to imitate our actions. The habits of a monkey are fixed, so it is therefore a conformist.

The monkey also has the aspect of a ram; it can be pushy, and when sufficiently enraged, a batterer. Monkeys and apes are also deceptive. They can be trouble-makers that may do irrevocable harm.

In the positive sense, an imitator is something that reflects. The reflection may be like a passive, clear mirror, or like the moon on a grander scale. At a high state of consciousness, it is a metaphor for the clear mirror or moon aspect of the mind.

The eye of the needle has been a favourite metaphor of the ancient Sages and philosophers since time immemorial. On the physical plane, the significance of the "eye" was explained under *A'yin* ע. The integration of false knowledge through what one perceives can make one act like a monkey, ape or ram. The needle portion of the metaphor is attributed to direction and guidance. It is like a pointer, compass or arrow. As a navigational instrument, the signpost measurements are angular – a key to passing through the eye of the needle.

The point of a needle is a reference to something that may torment, like anything else that is a trouble-maker. Sometimes it may be so small as to be unseen, like a sliver. Yet it may cause as much pain as being caught in a thornbush. Metaphysically, the point of a needle can leave on one's mind the same sharp engraving that it may leave on a gemstone.

Metaphysically, in order for one to pass through the eye of the needle, one must have a calm, clear and concentrated mind. The other side is a clear mirror image.

The Book of Creation states that "He enthroned Qof ק in sleep". Sleep in this context is a purely metaphysical metaphor. When one sleeps, one is inactive and inert. However when one's physical activities cease and one is silent, one dreams, and dreams are a reflection of one's subconscious.

The range of meanings for the Hebrew symbol Qof ק are poignant, from monkey/ape to eye of the needle, to sleep. They reflect the shift from conscious to unconscious, physical to spiritual. They are all metaphorical reflectors at the various levels of one's mind.

ר

RESH/ROSH Resh ר is the twentieth Hebrew symbol and the sixth of the seven "doubles". It is one of the few Hebrew symbols that has a clear double pronunciation by way of its full spelling. Its symbolic number is two hundred.

The "e" in Resh is pronounced as an "a", as in the word "able". The other spelling and pronunciation is the complementary portion of the double. Both are correct; however metaphysically, Rosh is more direct than Resh.

The Hebrew spelling of Rosh appears as ראש (rosh aleph shin). The spelling of Resh appears as רי"ש (resh yod shin). The change in vowels for ראש (rosh aleph shin) are also pronounced Resh. The difference is inconsequential, except for meditation purposes.

Both spellings and pronunciations have a multiplicity of the same meanings. For metaphysical purposes, the words head, beginning and tributary are the ones upon which we will concentrate. For now, we shall use the pronunciation of Rosh. The word first appears in Hebrew Scriptures in GEN II:10:

> And a river went out of Eden to water the garden; and from thence it was parted and became four heads.

וְנָהָר יֹצֵא מֵעֵדֶן לְהַשְׁקוֹת אֶת־הַגָּן
וּמִשָּׁם יִפָּרֵד וְהָיָה לְאַרְבָּעָה רָאשִׁים:

In the archetypal form of beginning— at birth— the head is the first to arrive and the first to discover. Similarly, when the soul leaves the body at death, it also carries with it certain aspects of the subconscious mind. This is also a beginning or birth – a first to arrive and discover.

Metaphysically, the beginning is clean and fresh and is linked to the source which is often called the fountainhead. A fountainhead is from the source of running water. It is not independent, but only a branch that receives its energy and force from a main body. The tributary nevertheless has the energy to bestow and reward. This is expressed in the Hebrew Scriptures through sacrifice and worship. The action of the two bring bountiful rewards.

Resh ר has a meaning that does not appear for the word Resh רֵישׁ (rosh yod shin) — the added denotation of poverty. This is not the poverty of physical necessities, but rather the weakness or lack of energy (both physical and mental) from which there is no apparent escape. This weakness is what keeps one on the cycle of life/death, death/life. This condition of the mind state is expressed in this particular Hebrew symbol.

The Book of Creation states that "He enthroned Resh ר in fruitfulness". Metaphysically, fruitful means prolific, which in turn implies an increase or expansion. This expansion may be smooth, have growing pains, or a combination of both. Prolific also has the metaphysical meaning of rich, fertile, or lush. Actions that are rich, fertile or lush have a better chance of success and completion than those which are arid and dry.

When one's heart and mind are fruitful, they are the first to discover whether the cycle is at the end of the beginning, or the beginning of the end.

SHIN/SIN

Shin ש ש is the twenty-first Hebrew symbol, and is one of the three "Mothers". It is also one of the main three Gates of Purification in Hebrew Qabbal teaching. Its symbolic number is three hundred.

Shin ש ש also has a dual pronunciation. When the symbol has a dot over the upper right hand side, ש (Shin), the pronunciation is "shin". When the dot appears over the upper left hand side, ש (Sin), the pronunciation is "sin". The "s" is soft in the former, and sharp in the latter.

Shin ש with this vowel configuration means *which, who, since,* and *seeing that.* There are two ways in which it may be spelled out: שן (shin nun) is the common Western Mystery method, which means tooth, jaw, or peak.

The metaphysical significance of the first spelling, the word tooth, infers something sharp, which also points the way. Since the tooth is sharp, it has the ability to pierce, or to break through things. This meaning of Shin was the Victorian-age manner of attempting to connect the Hebrew symbol and fire to a metaphysical understanding.

If one stretches the subconscious mind in terms of a tooth or peak, one may sense something of what the word means. Fire can point the way; like a tooth it can be sharp to the touch. It also has the destructive power to break through. In their physical forms, a peak is at the top edge of a tooth as well as fire. The fire of the Hebrew Qabbal is not the ordinary flame of common fire, nor is it a metaphor for the fire of the sun. While the fire energy of the sun is a physical necessity of life for all plants, animals, birds, and mankind, the fire of Shin ש is the metaphor for the latent energy of all primordial powers of energy inherent in the cosmic forces. This energy fire is a reflection of cosmic consciousness. Shin ש is also the symbol for the commencement of human physical form.

Matter, or even a miniscule portion of matter is the store-house of enormous energy. This inexhaustible energy comes from the eternal source. This energy fire originates beyond our relative world. It originates beyond the parts of our solar system that one may see and not see, beyond man's intellectual and scientific horizons.

At this stage of involution or evolution (coming into being, or passing away) Shin ש is in a state of inertia, that is asleep.

The Hebrew Qabbal composition of Shin ש is a Zayin ז Yod ' Vav ו, sitting on an inverted triangle . This fire energy from the Cosmic Universe is a gift from the single imageless Creator.

The Book of Creation states that "He enthroned Shin ש in fire", one of the creative forces. One of the three Mothers.

ת תּ
TAV

Tav תת is the twenty-second, and final Hebrew symbol. It is the seventh of the seven "doubles". It is pronounced with a short "o", as in "opposite". Its symbolic number is four hundred.

When Tav contains a dot in its centre it is pronounced T. Conversely without the centre dot it is pronounced S or Th.

The symbol Tav by itself has no meaning, is spelled out תו (tav vav), and pronounced Tav.

The Hebrew word Tav תו means a mark, and by implication a signature.

In its bluntest intellectual form, a mark sets a limit or a direction. It can become an objective destination or target. When one plumbs the depth of a destination or target, one seeks out its nature, character and quality. Each of these has a degree, shading and nuance.

Tav metaphysically is a major stepping stone or rung. Its place as the twenty-second symbol signifies a completion, like the rounding out of a circle or sphere. As a final symbol, it occupies a place of importance. To dedicated Hebrew Qabbal students, it may even be a spot of urgency or priority.

Since a mark is something that stands out of the ordinary, it implies a uniqueness. Tav ת is the "end of the line". If the preceding symbols are tools for the raising of one's state of consciousness, when one approaches the end, many questions arise.

Is this the final result? Has one graduated? Is this the climax of the Scriptural reference to the angels ascending and descending?

Are there any traces or evidence of a continuum?

If Aleph א is the first symbol and Tav ת the last, is there a metaphysical relationship between them?

If one puts the first and last symbols together תא (tav aleph) one gains the English meaning "make a mark". If one reverses them, את (aleph tav) one has the English meaning "a sign". Both have the same basic metaphysical meaning.

Just as importantly, if one adds the numerical values of Aleph א and Tav ת together, one discovers:

Aleph	א	=	1
Tav	ת	=	400
Total		=	401
Simplified Number	4 + 1	=	5

PEACE שָׁלוֹם

---

[4] The date ascribed to this early text is between the third and sixth century c.e. It contains six chapters, and about 1600 words, and was originally transmitted orally from teacher to student. It is considered by many to be one of the cornerstones of Qabbal teaching, yet owing to its gnostic, rather than religious nature, it was long considered to be "secret" information. In any event, it is plainly a work of visionary proportions that speaks in metaphor.

The Geometry of
the Hebrew Symbols

In the foregoing section of this book, it was pointed out that colour is symbolic of the mind of the Creator, and the Hebrew symbols are symbolic of the voice. Geometry is the counterpart, the handwriting.

It will be recalled that the first nine Hebrew symbols are associated with distinct geometric configurations, and that each has its own metaphysical interpretation that complements the symbol with which it is associated. Moreover, each configuration is an accumulative step in the development of those following it: in other words, they continue to build upon the previous ones. As will be seen in this chapter, the final stage of all the geometric representations together form what is metaphysically referred to as the Tree of the Knowledge of Good and Evil (opposites).

The nine individual steps that evolve in the geometry arising from Aleph א through Teth ט denote the Gnostic Hebrew Qabbal theme of the *completion of a cycle*. This metaphysically signals a transition from form to non-form (the latter almost exclusively belonging to the meditative sphere of experience).

Geometric configurations
and their significance:

Dot (Aleph) א

The eternal presence of absolute being is symbolized by a dot: it is elusive, mysterious and not perceptible to our physical senses. We may describe the dot as the cosmic point where the spiritual and physical come into being, and the vanishing point where the visible and invisible part company.

Other metaphysical symbols of this theme are the drop, pinhead and mustard seed. Words often used to exemplify this principle are monad and nebula, which denote infinite dimensions (and dimensionlessness), as well as infinite potential.

It may also be considered to be the point of transition between subconscious and conscious existence, as it lies in potentiality, before the moment of coming into being.

Two dots joined by an interconnecting line (Beth) ב

The mysterious, invisible presence of absolute being now *commences* to take absolute form. The two dots or monads with the interconnecting line, however do not have structural stability, and cannot hold two- or three-dimensional form. Metaphysically they are said to be at rest, and motionless.

This geometric representation of Beth denotes the separation of one into two, and relative form. The previous single dot splits into duality and creates *one dimension* (note that four points define three dimensions, five, *four* dimensions, and so on...)

The equal arm triangle (Gimmel) ג

An equal arm triangle represents the metaphysics of life's pulsation in motion. The third arm has stabilized the first two arms (the second created by the addition of a third point to the first two that arose from Aleph and Beth). And a perceptible form comes into being. The first two portions of the geometry have evolved through the triangle. It now has harmonious balance as evidenced by the third arm conjoining the others.

Fixed form requires/denotes duality, as well as balanced, objective thought.

The square (Daleth) ⊓

The square is the geometric symbol of uniform material knowledge. Because the sides of a square are always equal, one may say that the square represents equal, objective thought. The proportions of the dimensions of a square are unchangeable if it is to remain a square.

Metaphysically, the square can be a passage for just, righteous thought. It can also contain the blocks of an unchangeable, closed mind (one recalls the inherent duality of Gnostic Hebrew Qabbal themes).

The square is also geometrically composed of two right-angled isosceles triangles, containing a further connotation of balance that has firm support or stability.

The circle (Hé) ⊓

The circle represents clear awareness of spiritual eternity. It contains more scope than the material square. It contains the significance of "Behold! It is seen!"

As the sum of all the universe(s), it denotes completion and wholeness. It encompasses the entirety of Creation. At Creation, the circle had a beginning, however afterwards, circles and cycles are said to have no beginning and no end.

Geometrically the circle is the most efficient container of space in terms of its circumference and what may be contained within.

The rectangle

The rectangle is a symbol of knowledge that may be false, or knowledge that contains both truth and falsity: in other words, the truth has been bent. More often than not, the jagged edges are not recognizable.

Interlocking triangles (Vav) ‍ו

Two interlocking triangles (one pointing up, the other down) are the symbol of a being's male and female energies in balanced equilibrium or harmony. It is known as the Star of David, or the Seal of Solomon.

Inner square (Zayin) ‍ז

The perimeter of the inner square automatically equals the circumference of the large circle. It is added to the composite geometric pattern that has evolved through the preceding figures attached to their corresponding Hebrew symbols. (Zayin adds an inner square and seven inner circles to the overall picture). This symbolizes the unfolding of inner sight that allows one to see clearly on both material and spiritual levels.

In addition, the area of the circle (esoteric) is larger than the area of the *small square* (exoteric), symbolizing that the truths contained within the symbol of the circle are always larger than the truth contained within the symbol of the small square: the magnitude of the subconscious far exceeds that of the conscious mind.

It will be recalled that the symbolic number of Zayin is seven. One can only approximate a seven-sided figure.

Seven small circles

These are the geometric symbols of the spheres of the Universe(s), and Cosmic Truth(s) that is (are) contained within it. They denote fulfillment and happiness on the spiritual plane of consciousness. The seven small circles have a parallel flavoring with the inner square.

Pyramid (Het) ‍ח

The pyramid with its apex upward is the geometric symbol of the Northern Hemisphere. If the apex pointed downward the symbolism would indicate the Southern Hemisphere. The upward apex contains the metaphysical significance of the positioning of the earth in relation relative to the rest of the solar system.

At this stage of Gnostic Hebrew Qabbal geometry it is said that the balanced gate has been completed and opened and it is now up to the practitioner to pass through.

The pyramid is a metaphysical representation of the spiritual insight of the Northern Hemisphere in which the majority of readers live.

The symbolic number of Het is eight, and this also contains a significance of an eight-sided figure or octahedron. An octahedron is comprised (outwardly) of eight equal-sided triangles, where the upper part of the figure mirrors the lower – or two pyramids that share a common base, with one pointing upwards, the other downwards.

The Sephiroth (Teth) 𐤈

The ten Sephiroth are the geometric symbols of the main useable energy centres that lie within each human being.

They complete the complex geometric pattern that in Gnostic Hebrew Qabbal symbology illustrates the "Tree of the Knowledge of Good and Evil" (opposites).

Each of the ten Sephiroth are joined by a series of paths, and, in geometry, lines, which in turn represent the Hebrew symbols.

Geometric symbolism is hardly the exclusive property of Gnostic Hebrew Qabbal themes. The *gnostic* aspects are present in Nature, and much of what has been elaborated upon in this book is a direct reflection of what has surrounded and been a part of mankind since the "Beginning". Man and Nature are so intertwined as to be inseparable. Paradoxically, mankind's quest for self-discovery, along with an insatiable curiosity to unravel the mysteries of Nature invariably leads to an ultimate perception of this intertwining – and more.

A
•

Step 1

Start with a dot "A" near the top of your work space.

The dot marked A is the geometric representation
of the Hebrew symbol Aleph.

A
•

Step 2

With A as the centre,
use a compass to draw an arc
well down the workspace.

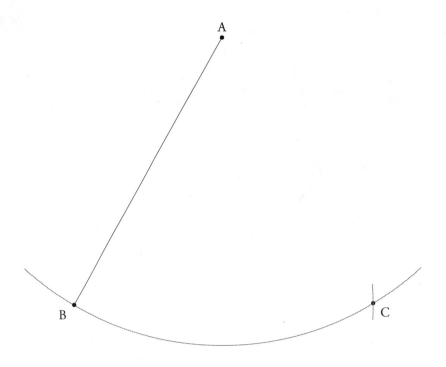

Step 3

Select a point on the arc and mark it "B" as shown above. With B as the centre and using the radius BA, cut the arc as shown above and designate the intersection as "C". Join line AB.

Two dots joined by the interconnecting line AB is the geometric representation of the Hebrew symbol Bayt.

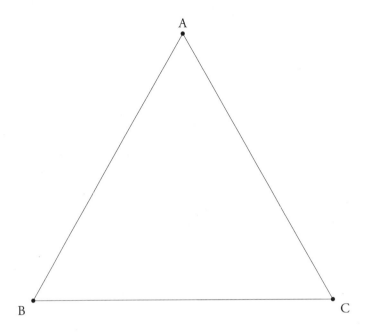

Step 4

Draw three straight lines connecting A to B, B to C and A to C.
The figure A:B:C is an equilateral triangle.

The equilateral triangle is the geometric representation of the
Hebrew symbol Gimmel.

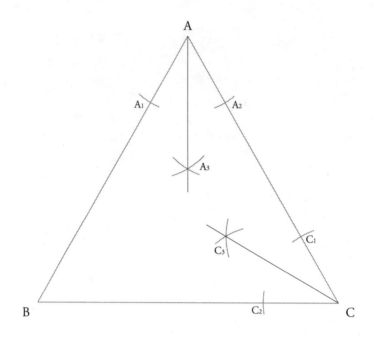

Step 5

We now bisect the angles at both A and C.
To bisect the angle A, draw small arcs from A to cut A:B and A:C
at A_1 and A_2. Using A_1 and A_2 as centres, draw two more arcs
intersecting the triangle at A_3.
To bisect the angle C, draw small arcs from C to cut C:A and
C:B at C_1 and C_2. Using C_1 and C_2 as centres, draw two more
arcs intersecting the triangle at C_3.
Draw a line from A through A_3 and C through C_3
as shown above.

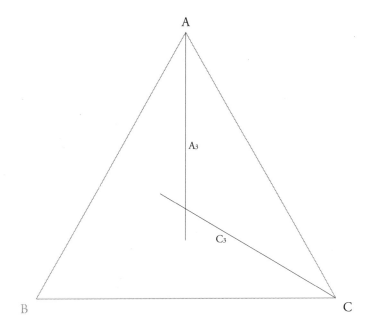

Step 6

Extend A:A₃ to intersect C:C₃ as shown above.

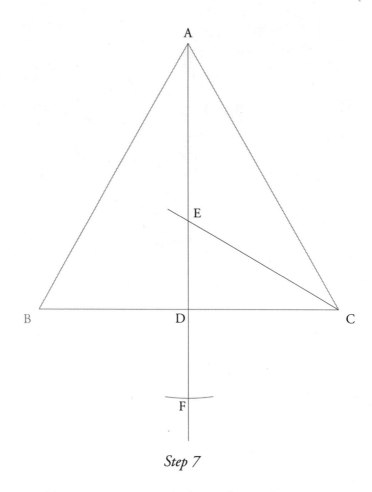

Step 7

Extend bisector A to meet the base of triangle A:B:C at D.
Mark the intersection of line A:D and C:E.
With centre D and radius E:D cut an arc at F. Extend E:D to F.

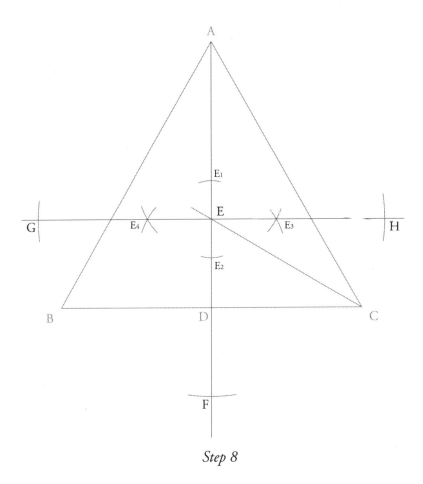

Step 8

From the centre E,
we will now draw a new line at right angles to A:F.
Place the compas point at E and draw an arc to cut the line A:F
above and below E at E_1 and E_2. Extend the compas points further and use centre E_1 and E_2 for two arcs each,
intersecting at points E_3 and E_4.
Extend E:E_4 to equal the length A:E. Extend E:E_3 to equal the
length A:E. Designate end points as
G and H as shown above.

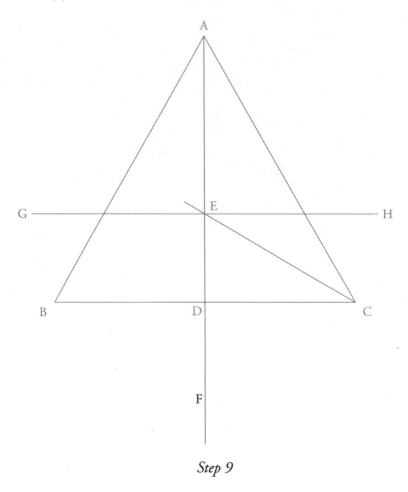

Step 9

Extend line D:F downwards. (Be careful that A:E:D:F is a single
line). Lines B:C, G:H should be parallel
when this step is finished.

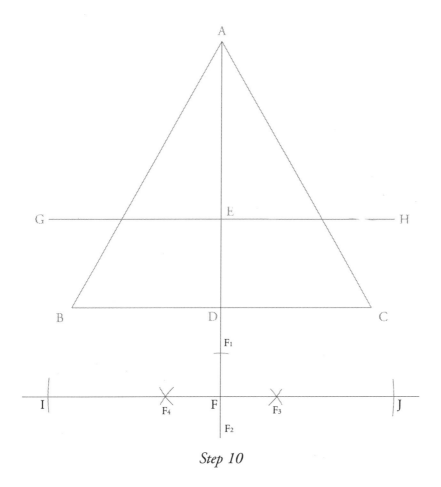

Step 10

Place the compass point at F and draw arcs to cut line D:F at F₁
and F extended downwards at F₂. Extend compass points a bit
further and use centres F₁ and F₂ to create F₃ and F₄. Join
F₃ and F₄ and extend. Place compass point at A and set compass
at radius A:E. With compass point on point F and
radius A:E cut F₃:F₄ at I and J.

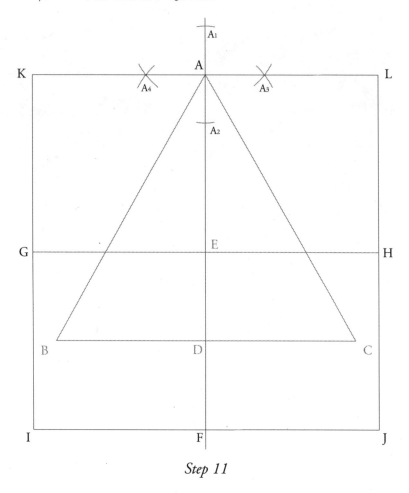

Step 11

Extend line A:E upwards. Place the compass point at A and cut
arcs A₁ and A₂ as shown above. Extend the compass points
a bit further and using A₁ and A₂ as centres, create A₃ and A₄.Join
A₃:A₄. Place compass point at A and extend to AE. Cut A₃:A₄
at K and L. Draw lines K:L, K:I, I:J, L:J.

I:J:K:L is a square and is the geometric symbol of
the Hebrew symbol Daleth.

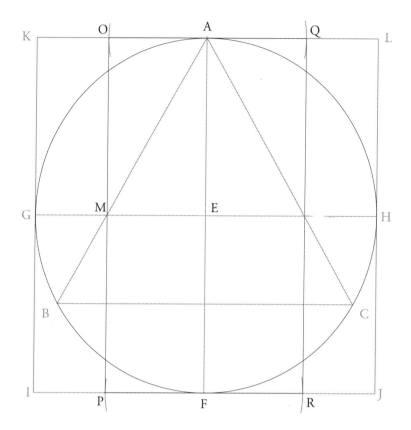

Step 12

Place the compass at E and extend compass to A. Draw circle as shown above, using E as centre point. The circumference of the circle should touch points A, G, B, F, C and H. Set compass point at E and extend to M. With this length and centre points A and F, cut arcs at O, P, Q and R. Connect O to P and Q to R. O:P:Q:R is a rectangle.

The circle and the rectangle are the geometric symbols of the Hebrew symbol Hey.
This is the golden rectangle.

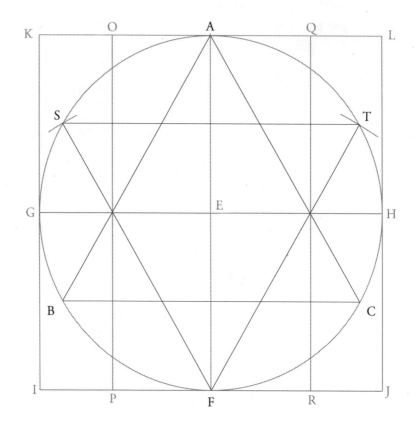

Step 13

Place compass point at A and extend compass to B. With this length place the compass point at F and cut arcs on the circle at S and T, as shown above. Join F to S, S to T and T to F. Triangles A:B:C and F:S:T are equal, equilateral and interlocked.

Interlocked, equilateral triangles are the geometric symbol of the Hebrew symbol Vav.

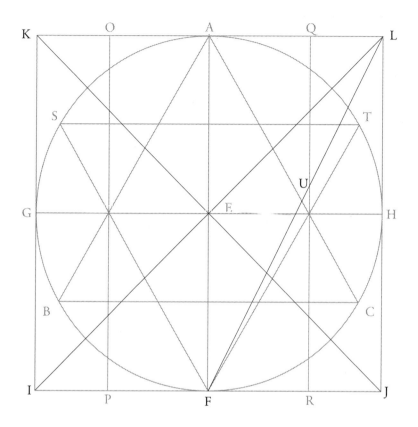

Step 14

Join L:I, K:J and L:F. L:F crosses Q:R at the point U.

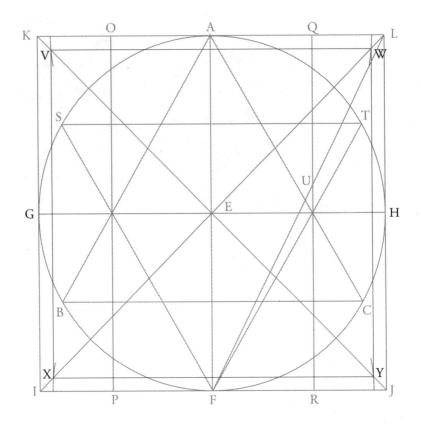

Step 15

With the centre A and the radius equal to Q:U, cut K:J at the
point V and L:I at the point W. With the centre at F and the
same radius, cut K:J at the point Y and L:I at the point X. Join V,
W, X, Y. The perimeter of the square V:W:X:Y is equal to the circumference of the circle with point E as the centre

The geometric square V:W:X:Y represents a portion of the
Hebrew symbol Zayin.

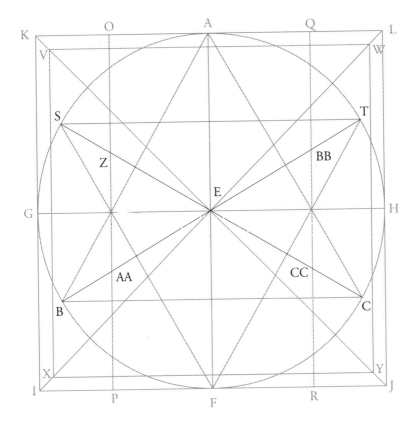

Step 16

Join B:E. B:E intersects O:P at AA.
Join S:E. S:E intersects O:P at Z
Join T:E. T:E intersects Q:R at BB
Join C:E. C:E intersects Q:R at CC.

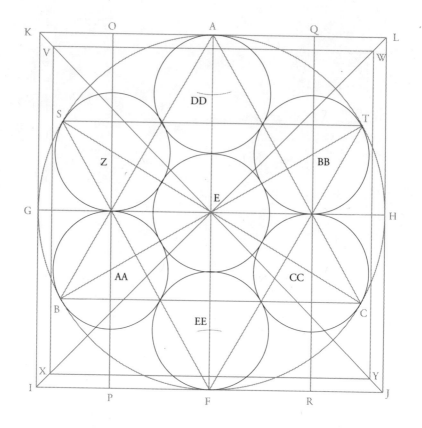

Step 17

With AA as centre and B:AA as radius, draw a circle. With Z as
centre and Z:S as radius, draw a circle. With the same radius and
centre at A, cut A:E at DD. Draw a circle at DD with the radius
A:DD. Draw a circle at BB with the radius BB:T. Draw a circle at
CC with the radius C:CC. With the same radius and centre at F,
cut F:E at EE. Draw a circle at EE with the radius F:EE. With
the centre E and the same radius draw a circle.

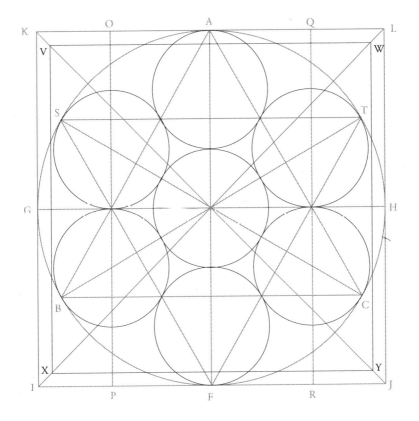

Step 18

The square V:W:X:Y and the seven circles are the geometric
symbols of the Hebrew symbol Zayin.

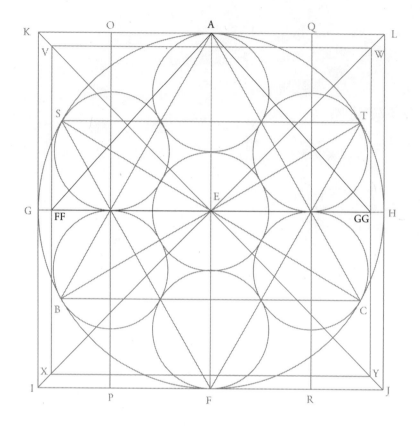

Step 19

Given that V:X intersects E:G at the point FF, join A:FF.
Similarly W:Y crosses E:H at the point GG. Join A:GG.
The triangle A:FF:GG is a pyramid.

The pyramid A:FF:GG is the geometric symbol of the
Hebrew symbol Het.

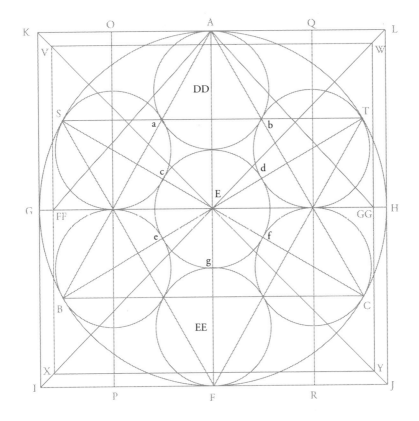

Step 20

Where S:T crosses A:B, mark it as "a", and where it crosses A:C, mark it as "b". Where S:E crosses the point where the two circles touch, mark it as "c". Where E:T crosses the point where the two circles touch mark it as "d". Similarly for E:B at point "e", E;F at point "g" and E"C at point "f"

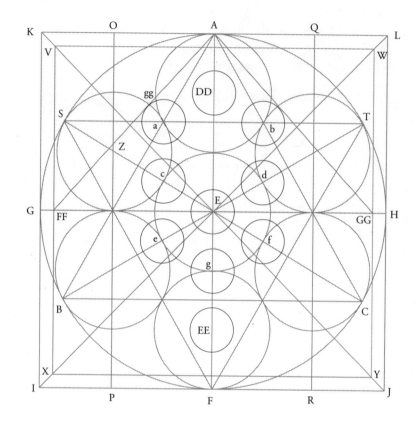

Step 21

Circle "a" intersects the line A:FF at "gg". With centre "a" and
radius to the line a:gg draw a circle. Using the same radius draw
circles using centres at b, c, d, e, f, g, DD, EE and E.

These are the ten Sephiroth of the
Tree of the Knowledge of Good and Evil.

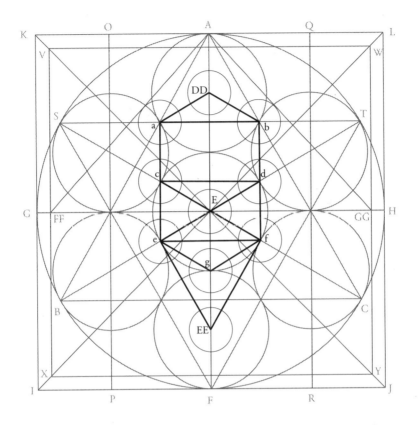

Step 22

Join DD to a, a to b, b to DD, a to c, b to d, c to d, DD to E,
c to e, c to E, d to E, d to f, e to E, E to f, E to g, e to EE,
f to EE, f to g, e to f, e to g and g to EE.

This completes the paths of energy of the
Tree of the Knowledge of Good and Evil.
It also corresponds to the Hebrew symbol Tayth.

There is no need to find a new world -
only to see the present one differently.
- Leslie Dawson, Master

In the beginning

The first verse of Hebrew Scriptures (GEN I:I), "In the beginning, God created the heavens and the earth", has been the subject of many different interpretations for thousands of years. The following is one which has evolved from the Hebrew Qabbal school of "Ruach-Ha-Kodesh" (The Path of the Holy Breath). This path has its spiritual roots in the metaphysical interpretations of Scriptures and the practice of meditation. It is important to note that this school does not hold that one teaching is necessarily the only Path of Truth for all. Therefore, what is presented here should be contemplated in the sense that it may be added to other teachings – those from the past, those currently being developed, and those which will appear in the future.

This school of thought makes the statement that "One does not attain the Path, but discovers it". In other words, the path is eternally *here*. As Leslie Dawson so aptly put it, "One finds it within one's body, within the senses, and within the world in which one lives". At the centre of this teaching is a central theme of love, compassion, wisdom and understanding, that may assist one in perceiving the present world in a deeper and more complete sense.

The Hebrew Qabbal interpretation of GEN I:I may be symbolized through the lighting of two white candles, and may be extended through the composition of candlesticks made of oak, brass, their bases, and flames. These are symbols of love, compassion, wisdom and understanding.

The base of the candlestick is composed of wood, which expresses the link between the physical (material) and non-physical worlds. This may also be used to signify the link between the formed and the formless. Some teachings use the words outer and inner, or exoteric and esoteric. This wooden base is made of oak, which has long been a symbol of strength, durability, tolerance and innate energy. In Hebrew Scriptures, the word for oak is "Elah" אֵלָה, which has been generally translated into English as "terebinth" אֵלָה שְׁמַנוּנִית.

Those of French, English, Scottish and Irish lineage may recognize that their heritage goes back to the Druids, whose rich and honoured teaching used the oak tree as the symbol for the highest form of physical human attainment. This is an example of an "archetype", an original pattern or model of all things of the same type, that goes back beyond living memory.

The brass of the candlestick which holds the candle is the symbol of life's activities on the physical plane. Since brass is not pure (it is made by fusing two base metals), it is a reminder that one is constantly watering down or blending one's pure spiritual potential. In other words, how often in the course of one's daily life does one combine the good with the not-so-good? Many of life's activities may be seen as being impure.

While modern candles are a composite of natural and synthetic materials, they were traditionally made of beeswax, which has the characteristics of being both hard and soft at the same time, principles which are in opposition. Although flexible, it sticks together and acts as a connector. Moreover, the beehive is made of this same material. It is a house which is further connected and built in opposites. The metaphysical significance of opposites that are connected and balanced is that of harmony, equilibrium and unity – significant themes in Hebrew Qabbal teaching.

Wax symbolizes the ability to dissolve or raise the physical to the spiritual (solid to fluid). In its natural form, beeswax is liquid, however it is solid in its candle form. Once again, this is an indication of opposites.

The white of the candles signifies the purest form of love and compassion on the physical plane.

The flame itself is the earthly symbol of esoteric light. Most Western Mystery teachings use the same symbolism. The Hebrew Qabbal teaches that Creation comes from light, and accordingly, the flame of the candle (fire) becomes identified with creation and all forms of life.

The flame of life is joined to the candles of love and compassion. It causes the solid physical form to liquify, which then vaporizes to smoke, going from the visible to the invisible. Smoke is the symbol of preserving and enhancement. The vaporized wax and smoke rise together, carrying the love, compassion, wisdom and understanding of humanity into the eternal cosmic universe, which we commonly call heaven. In this way, the physical source in its spiritual form returns to the cosmos, the source of Creation.

Two flaming candles have a further inner Hebrew Qabbal meaning. Two is the symbolic number of the second Hebrew symbol, Beth ‎ב.

The Hebrew symbols, their numerical values, colours and geometry are all interlocked and inter-related. Individually, each expresses outer and inner meanings. An individual may readily respond with insight and revelation to one form of symbol but not another. The Ancient Hebrew Sages molded symbols such as the two candles into a veiled mysterious representation, which in this case happens to be a metaphor for the Hebrew symbol Beth ‎ב.

One may trace a line that progresses, in rising order, to the singular inner meaning of the two candlesticks, whose imagery and symbolism start at the oak wood base, and move through the brass, candles, flame, and vaporized smoke, to the heavens. This metaphor commences in physical form, and is completed in the spiritual, unformed. We can also find this singular line of progression in reverse, which can commence, in descending order, from the source of Creation — from the beginning.

The Hebrew symbol Beth ב by itself looks simple and peaceful, and very much like any consonant in a foreign alphabet. However, as can be seen from the foregoing chapter on the Hebrew symbols, it conceals a treasure of meanings.

As has been stated previously, when Beth ב is opened up and spelled out using further Hebrew symbols, we discover that one of its meanings is a house, something stationary, without motion, solid, and having longevity. In ancient times, a house was built of stone and stood for an enormous length of time. It was often inhabited for generations by the descendants of the same family. So, it follows that a house also has the meaning of solidity and lineage, as in the House of David. To build the house, a foundation was laid at rest, and the material for the foundation came from a natural source – as it does to this day.

Metaphysically, Beth ב may be said to be something that has been brought to rest, and this is the basic metaphysical theme that lies within the two flaming candlesticks.

The geometric representation of Beth ב, two dots or nebulae joined by an interconnecting line, should be thought of as two whirlwinds – with a centre, but no defined outer boundaries. As previously indicated, in modern terms, they could be thought of as two connected molecules which compose salt — a very prominent commodity in Biblical times, and one of the fundamental necessities of life.

It should be abundantly apparent that all Hebrew symbols have an abstract quality, but they are very flexible and contain a duality of meanings. In fact, each is a condition or state of consciousness. Each is a conductor of energy that represents a positive and negative condition of consciousness.

Modern language uses various words to describe these opposing conditions: positive and negative, active and passive, wholesome and unwholesome. These words crop up in various teachings and philosophies. One should not take them literally or at face value, as that can be misleading.

The Book of Creation, written more than 1500 years ago, mentioned in the analysis of the symbols, was among the finest esoteric works ever produced on the subject. In its statement that "He enthroned Beth ב in life", it was pointing up the metaphysical concept that life is the archetype of all dwellings. The circle, so to speak, is closed. One has made a complete circle from two candlesticks through the Hebrew symbol Beth ב, to life, the archetype of all physical dwellings.

Metaphysically, the word dwelling denotes more than the physical body. Hebrew Qabbal teaching indicates that life is also the spirit and the soul within the body, within a container. It is the vital force that we call spiritual. Once again, this invokes duality; one's physical and spiritual presence are one within the other.

Like the stone house of old, life's foundation comes from the source, the fountainhead, and it resides within the temple in the body. Something that comes from the Source is from the place of origin, from the beginning, from Genesis.

Beth ב is the symbol of this concept. It combines the life giving energy from the Source with the initial instance of taking on form. It is the indescribable point of conception – there, but not active. It is a point where form commences, but where there is no motion.

At this stage of conception everything that comes into being has duality. Instantly there is the presence of a spiritual and physical being. This unit contains one's consciousness and subconsciousness. It contains all the initial foundations from one's past, for the present and future thoughts, emotions and concepts. Each of these in their own right contain the duality of opposites. Contemporary language would say that the essence of one's ego or psyche is established to work in opposition (duality) with one's spiritual body as an alter ego. The point of conception contains inherent duality. It arises or takes its form from the source – fountainhead, and resides in the purest archetypal dwelling – the womb.

Hebrew Qabbal teaching, through the letter Beth ב, recognizes that at the point of conception, one arrives with two bodies, one physical, and one spiritual. One has, in the beginning, an ego/psyche entity that shares the same space with a spiritual entity. The essence of this spiritual entity contains all the energy of the cosmic universe that commences with the Creator. Without this duality, one could not exist. It is this duality that creates the structure from which one can recognize the physical world. One requires the opposites in order to have a point of reference from which one may set out. One could not recognize pleasure unless one knew pain; one cannot know good unless one knows evil. Hebrew Scriptural teachings are filled with duality, and these commence in GEN I with heaven and earth, the spiritual, as opposed to the physical. It continues through the evolution of mankind, using duality as its illustration.

The duality of the Hebrew symbols is the source of much confusion in Biblical interpretation. Each symbol, and consequently, each word can have a positive and a negative meaning. While each symbol expresses a condition or state of consciousness, it indicates the concomitant growth of life experience and spirituality. One may say that each symbol is a set of energies flowing in two directions at the same time. A poignant example of this is the fact that from the moment of birth, one's physical form (even while maturing) is deteriorating, while the spiritual aspect is increasing and becoming enhanced.

So far we have illustrated that Beth ב is the indescribable point of conception, where form commences but there is no motion. It is a point where the spiritual and physical first come into union, and the source is the fountainhead – the place of original creation, from the beginning of Genesis. If this is so, one should be able to find the letter Beth ב near GEN I:1 in the Hebrew Scriptures. In fact, it is the first symbol, of the first word, that starts GEN I:1, and the first symbol of the second word as well. The first three symbols in Hebrew Scriptures, Beth ב/Resh ר /Aleph א are defined as *to create* or *to make*. This should be thought of in the widest cosmic sense possible. The second three symbols, Shin ש/Yod י/Tav ת, mean *to place a foundation,* as well as *dress* or *garment*. The second word repeats the first three symbols of the first word. Whatever language into which the Hebrew is translated, the words used are "in the beginning".

One might ask, "Why don't Hebrew Scriptures start with the first Hebrew symbol, Aleph א rather than with Beth ב?" The Ancient Hebrew Sages were consciously aware of the point at which spiritual essence comes into initial union with physical form. It was a rather brilliant way of avoiding the nearly impossible task of attempting to explain the single imageless Creator.

Nor did they start at the point where the earth and mankind were already functioning. They chose the most subtle of subtle places, the almost unfathomable point where the spiritual and the physical come into being and eventually mature into form. It is the Scriptural starting point for all that was, is, or will be within the Cosmic Universe. It is at the same time the starting point of the planet we call Earth. At the instant of the union of the spiritual and human bodies, all of the dualities are in place. All of the dualities, the opposites, that one needs to support one's life systems are in potential to be put into motion: the dualities of pleasure and pain, anima and animus, hot and cold, wholesomeness and unwholesomeness, black and white, light and darkness, the material and the spiritual. Most people feel that their spiritual essence is quite elusive. However, no matter what race, creed, colour or sex in which one enters the world, one's "Beginning" contains the same set of dual ingredients whose origins are the same Source.

If this teaching has a logical, intellectual and intuitive aspect, the first Hebrew symbol, Aleph א, should be quite near to "the beginning", and it is. The third word in GEN I:I, commences with Aleph א– "Elohim" אֱלֹהִים (God).

As was discussed in the metaphysical analysis of the symbol itself, Aleph has no vocalization unless it is accompanied by an attached vowel. Alone it has no meaning, other than signifying the number one. Spelled out, it has the meanings — to associate, learn, teach, cow, ox, oxen (in the sense of yoking or taming), a thousand, or bringing forth thousands. In metaphysical teaching, bringing forth thousands indicates the infinite, untold or limit-less. In modern analytical language, a thousand, however, is finite.

The yoking or taming of an ox/oxen, indicates that Aleph א is both singular and plural. Again, this illustrates duality. The significance of a cow or an ox is also a metaphysical metaphor for members of mankind who are in the power of untamed material self-indulgence.

The geometric configuration for Aleph א is a single monad, similar to the monads of Beth ב, which are like whirlwinds or nebulae – circular, but without defined form. In this circular form, it has no beginning and no end. It has no point of definition, and no substance. Although the geometrical configura-tion is a monad or dot, it is abstract and dimensional.

The following shows spirit as symbolized by Aleph א:

> It is like air
>
> It is breath
>
> It is the soul
>
> It is the vital force that allows us to live
>
> It has no substance
>
> It is abstract
>
> It is infinite and immortal
>
> It is all that is and all that is not
>
> It is ignorance of fear
>
> It is the everlasting flame of life
>
>
> Its origin is from the Source
>
> The Greeks called it Pneuma
>
> The Hindus and Buddhists call it Prana

In the Hebrew Scriptures, it is "Ruach" רוּחַ, as in Genesis I:2, "and the *spirit* of God hovered over the face of the waters". Another example is in GEN VIII:15, "And they went in unto Noah in the ark, two and two of all flesh wherein is the *breath of life*." The Hebrew word for breath in these examples is "Ruach" רוּחַ which means breath or whirlwind, and by resemblance, spirit.

The spirit/breath of life is the main factor of balancing one's inner energies. Used properly, it can bring life's vital forces into balanced equilibrium or harmony. The spirit/breath of life is the direct representation of God from whence Creation comes. It is the cosmic energy that is everywhere, all at one time. It energizes and gives life to every living creature.

Another illustration of the differences between Aleph א and Beth ב is to express Aleph א as being active, and Beth ב as passive. This is a subtle difference, as Aleph א, being active, is from whence it comes – Creation. Beth ב being passive, inactive, is where the creative principle comes to rest. Aleph א must exist before Beth ב, and Beth ב emerges from the actions of Aleph א. The inactive substance with an eternal soul, formed from the breath of life, represents the Creator from whence Creation comes – the conduit through which the creative forces from the Source are brought into form. This is the moment of conception.

Scriptures start with the occurrence of something tangible, at a place that mankind can understand. To render it mysterious, it has been turned inside out. It is incumbent upon mankind to make it productive.

One
which contains Two

The Hebrew Qabbal theme of "One which contains Two" is the concept that the human being is a dynamic of opposing forces constantly seeking to find what is often referred to as *balanced equilibrium* or *balanced harmony*. These "two" opposing forces are constantly seeking to find balance within one's "One" inner self.

Most people view themselves as a single identity, with a solid body. In reality, one is a combination of two opposing forces that are in conflict. These opposing forces, contained in what appears to be a single body, are energies that are at war, and the ongoing sets of conflicts are what we sense as suffering.

As mentioned earlier, the twenty-two Hebrew symbols have this special dual quality. The language and writings that they form automatically inherit the same dual abstract meanings. This can create confusions amid Hebrew Scriptural interpretations — one may be positive, another negative; one may refer to an inner, spiritual plane, another to a purely materialistic or sensual one. Some interpretations even mix the two.

Each individual is a unique container of dual opposing forces with its own special blend. A part of spiritual growth is the self-discovery of these opposing forces which are in a state of conflict. Spiritual and/or psychological growth begins when one seeks to refine them into an integral state of balanced harmony.

In the metaphysical sense, the theme of "One which contains Two" commences prior to GEN I:1. It is ongoing, continuous, and shares a common thread with all the world's major philosophies. References may be found in the writings of Freud and Jung, Plato, Tibetan Buddhist Tantric teachings, the Tao, the various Yogas, Gnosticism, Alchemy and even Mystical Astrology.

We will expand upon the Gnostic Hebrew Qabbal understanding of Creation and "duality". These teachings assert that in the beginning all space, all universes were void. However these unformed and void universes contained an *unimaginable* white light which in Hebrew Qabbal teaching is called "AIN".

The first act of Creation was the singular withdrawal or contraction of this indescribable white light from infinite space. It withdrew into an infinitesimal point of pure energy. This withdrawal or contraction is called "AIN-SOPH" — that is limitless and boundless and beyond intellectual comprehension.

The second act of Creation was that out of this withdrawal or contraction came a single ray of pure white light that was shot into primordial space. This indescribable ray of light gave life to the soupy void, and is called "AIN-SOPH-OR". It is often referred to as the *"splendour of a flash of lightning"*.

This act of Creation is still ongoing, and it is interesting to note that modern science explains the above as the "Big Bang" theory. After the initial "explosion", sufficient cooling took place so that substance or matter could form: the forming of the basic particles of matter. This forming of substance would correspond to the AIN-SOPH-OR.

The ancient Hebrew Sages went one step further. They not only explained how matter was formed, but also that with the formation of matter came a vital force – the eternal soul.

We have already explored how the Hebrew symbol Beth ב expresses this duality of action, as it symbolizes both physical and spiritual formation at conception. At the point of original Creation, the universe and the Earth contained a sacred soul and physical form as well. It expresses the concept that form takes place through the action of *two* opposing forces: one force is form itself, the other the spiritual body. These opposing forces are with us as we physically enter this world.

The Hebrew Sages encapsulated the duality of humanity in GEN I:27, "and God created man(kind) in his own image, in the image of God created he him; male and female created he them".

The concept for the soul/spirit comes from the third word in GEN I:1, "Elohim" אֱלֹהִים (God), whose first letter is the Hebrew symbol Aleph א, which denotes *spirit*. This dualism is part of every person's nature. As one continues with spiritual study and practice, one's awareness increases. Eventually one may clearly see that there are two sides to the pulling apart, actions in opposition – dualism. It holds one back from becoming whole, becoming one. The battle ebbs and flows, and there seems to be no clear winning side.

Biologically, our organisms function properly when they are in balanced harmony. If one organ is disrupted, it affects others. When this happens, various healing techniques are used in an attempt to make the organ whole, and to return it to balanced harmony with the rest of the organism. Unfortunately, the healing of one's psyche is more intimately related to the theme of *one which contains two*.

So far, we have discussed where this dualism originated. The next step is to examine why it is so elusive, and what *wholeness* really entails.

We find that in GEN I:1, "In the beginning God Created..." in the following order:

LIGHT: He divided it from darkness and called light day and darkness night.

FIRMAMENT: He divided the waters from the firmament. He gathered the waters in one place and let land appear.

EARTH: He let the earth put forth grass, herb yielding seeds and tree bearing fruit.

STARS: He created lights in the firmament to give light upon the earth.

SUN AND MOON: He created two great lights. One to rule by day and one to rule by night. There was evening and there was morning.

The living creatures of the waters. The *fowl* who fly above the earth... and *every living creature that creepeth*. The living creatures he brought them forth from the earth, *cattle* and *creeping things* and *beast of the earth* after its kind. "And God created man(kind) in his own image, *male and female created he them.*"
(A single identity which contains two, *paraphrased from* GEN I:27.)

The theme of duality lies in the first three words of GEN I:1 (which begin with the Hebrew symbols Beth ב/Beth ב/Aleph א) and then surfaces in the creation of a combined male/female. On the seventh day, God rested from his work.

GEN II:4 then goes on to say, "These are the generations of the heaven and of the earth when they were created" (GEN II:4). In metaphysical teaching the word "generations" means ages or eons.

The evolution of mankind, "Adam", continues. At this stage the male/female entity is dual but *formless*. Then in GEN II:7 we find "Then the Lord God formed man of the dust of the ground, and breathed into his nostrils the breath of life, and man became a living soul". It is still a dual male/female entity, but it has taken on form. It has also acquired a "living soul". We are introduced to two sets of duality in one container. One of the dual sets is physical and spiritual, the other male/female. The modern word for this state of consciousness is androgyny – "a balanced being in harmony within itself". Two sets of opposites in one.

Hebrew Scriptures then relate that this androgynous being was placed in a garden in Eden. In GEN II:22, the final act of mankind's physical evolution takes place when the male and female entities are separated – the third and final act of mankind's creation is complete. Their state of consciousness is still pure...

"and they were both naked, the man and his wife, and were not ashamed" (GEN II:25). Each individual, each single entity with its own "One Which Contains Two" is still in balanced harmony.

It is only after the male and female partake of the fruit from the "tree of the knowledge of good and evil" (which should be construed as the knowledge of opposites) that the war of duality is on. The separation of one's state of consciousness from the whole is complete. It is to this state of balanced harmony, this *oneness of androgyny*, that we wish to return. The memory of this balanced equilibrium is locked into one's eternal memory bank. It is elusive because it is not the *physical* state of androgyny to which one aspires, but the psychic or spiritual.

There is a Hebrew symbol that constantly reminds us of this challenge and pursuit, a desire to return to the wholeness that lies buried deep within one's primordial mind: it is the geometric sign of the interlocking triangles, commonly known as the Star of David, or the Seal of Solomon.

The above is simply an overview of the potential themes contained in Genesis, and barely touches the complexities that have been woven into this portion of the Hebrew Scriptures. The explanations contained herein are merely a "jumping off point" for further in-depth study.

T'rumah
the temple in the wilderness

The construction of the Temple in the Wilderness is one of the key Hebrew Scriptural teachings, whose inner meaning is hidden within the instructions given to Moses for building a portable sanctuary whose centre focus is the Ark of the Covenant.

As you read the following verses, EX XXV: 1-8, do so closely. Contemplate the choice of words that have been used to underscore the theme that appears at the very beginning of the passage.

> 1 And the Lord spoke unto Moses, saying:
> 2 'Speak unto the children of Israel, that they take for Me an offering; of every man whose heart maketh him willing ye shall take My offering. 3 And this is the offering which ye shall take of them: gold, and silver, and brass; 4 and blue, and purple, and scarlet, and fine linen, and goats' hair; 5 and rams' skins dyed red, and sealskins, and acacia-wood; 6 oil for the light, spices for the anointing oil, and for the sweet incense; 7 onyx stones, and stones to be set, for the ephod and for the breastplate. 8 And let them make Me a sanctuary, that I may dwell among them.

This teaching, in Hebrew, is called "T'rumah" תרומה, which denotes "something set apart" as a freely-given gift, or offering: (EX XXV:2)

...that they take for Me an offering; of every
man whose heart maketh him willing...

This is an inner teaching of creating a spiritual sanctuary and opening the heart in order to build a place of holiness within oneself.

To expand upon this theme, a basic structure that is portable (are we not?) may be built by anyone who can take this metaphysical lesson to heart and learn to develop the freedom to give from within. The word "willing" denotes a natural, spontaneous expression of an awakened heart that is balanced with the awakened mind. In this way one may experience the ultimate balance of Love and Compassion, Wisdom and Understanding.

Love and compassion alone are not enough – without wisdom and understanding they lead to blissful ignorance. Wisdom and understanding devoid of the balancing effects of love and compassion lead to arrogance. We have previously explored the themes of duality and opposites inherent in Gnostic Hebrew Qabbal teaching, and the themes presented in this Scriptural story are no different; the heart, and its gifts have two sides. In its positive aspect, the heart denotes essence, inner being, the centre, virtue, middle course, origin, immortality, vigorousness, perseverance, courage of one's convictions, spirit, love and compassion. Conversely, it can contain egotism, selfishness, passion, temper, prejudice, and the sense of being imprisoned. While on the physical material plane the heart is a vital organ necessary and central to life, on the metaphysical level it is related to a powerful esoteric energy centre. But just as the heart must also work in conjunction with the brain to coordinate physical existence, the heart centre must also be open and function correctly for one to have "eyes that see and ears that hear".

Modern social psychology would analyze arrogance as being the result of a lack of self-esteem; a fearful ego over-compensating in the opposite direction in order to delude others that the individual has self-confidence. The Ancient Hebrew Sages were supremely aware of the mind games humans play, their causes and reactions. Indeed, wouldn't it be more profitable for the arrogant individual to eliminate his fear rather than to cover it up with the illusion of see-through courage?

The story of T'rumah הרומה speaks of offering(s) of the heart, concealing them in material metaphors of gold, silver, brass... There are twenty-two gifts, just as there are twenty-two Hebrew symbols. Each material item or gift has its own inner metaphysical meaning that denotes an aspect of psychological or spiritual growth.

Some modern, everyday figures of speech that are familiar to all of us use heart imagery to infer certain aspects about individuals: a heart of gold, or heartless depict two very opposite states of mind.

The theme of willingness to give spontaneously and freely infers the liberation from the major block of fear. In contemporary terms, many people have a trepidation of being dumped on or of being taken advantage of. Some only give out of a sense of guilt. None of these mind-states are wholesome or profitable. Moreover, one cannot extort wholesome love from another by the giving of material goods, yet one can create some type of illusory attachment on the part of the recipient, usually greed.

Clearly, the Hebrew Sages intended one to contemplate one's rationale for giving. On a spiritual level, there may be a fear of letting go of the material, tangible, sense-driven aspects of the self in order to encounter a higher Truth.

One may explore the Gnostic Hebrew Qabbal understanding of the word *offering* in order to discover the positive and negative aspects of the items that are listed below from EX XXV: 1-8, along with their metaphysical or abstract essences.

1. GOLD: In the positive sense, gold denotes the highest level of concentrated wisdom and intelligence operating on the physical plane. It is the pure concentration of the spiritual essence through earthly wisdom. It also represents the omnipresent richness of finite matter whose source is universal thought substance. Gold is also considered to be white, malleable, priceless, unique, and pure. Other images associated with

gold are of euphoria, happiness and success.

In the negative sense, gold denotes egotism, self-centered-ness, narcissism, vanity, selfishness, opportunism, greed, and is indicative of visual fallacy (all that glitters is not gold).

2. SILVER: The positive aspects of silver are similar to those of gold, but a paler imitation. It denotes something that is euphoric, pure, white, malleable and happy. Its opposite values are of something debased, clipped and, in the sense of a forgery, infers false knowledge. Silver may be viewed as merely a plating or veneer, but is traditionally known in metaphysics as a product of good substance.

3. BRASS: The positive side of brass encompasses boldness, strength, substance, and musical vibrations, as well as being indicative of a superior teacher as a director or navigator. The obverse contains the sense of a watered-down mixture that is not pure, along with loudness, discord, friction, sauciness, dis-respect, impertinence and blatancy.

    Brass is metaphysically typified as life's activities. It is impure, as it is made by blending other metals which have their own esoteric meanings. The end result is a blend of each participant's strengths and weaknesses.

    It should be noted that gold, silver and the components of brass are found directly in the earth, or are naturally occurring minerals. They are shaped or purified through the use of fire, which is one of the three main gates of purification in Gnostic Hebrew Qabbal teaching.

4. LINEN: Hebrew Scriptures refer to this offering as "fine" linen, which denotes a process of refining, and in this case refers to the natural improvement, order and coherence of life's activi-ties. The negative metaphysical aspects of linen include vanity, pride, arrogance, boastfulness, disorder, non-coherence, and ultimately, the non-spiritual.

    In keeping with gnostic themes, the Ancient Hebrew

Sages specifically chose to use imagery evoked by linen, rather than cotton. Both materials are familiar, however linen has always been more highly valued as a more noble product. Costlier to produce and refine, and not as readily procured, linen has a hard, durable finish that has something of a sheen. Cotton fibres are lacklustre and dull.

5. GOATS' HAIR: In a positive sense, goats were valued for meat and dairy products, and their skins were often used to make rough outer clothing and containers. The goat is typically a symbol of resistance, restlessness, opposition, aggression and obstinacy (not to mention the fact that they smell bad).

   Metaphysically, the goat may signify vitality, vigour, life and cheerfulness. It is also esoterically linked to the theme of a place of refuge to which one may stubbornly cling.

6. RAMS' SKIN: In a positive sense, the ram may be seen as a pro-genitor of innocence, as well as providing products of suste-nance, much as the goat. However its association with the concepts of physical strength and willful anger (a pointer to the human ego), along with resistance to divine law, or an intention to undermine same, are all negatives.

   Any sort of skin may be metaphysically interpreted as a form of materiality that is shallow and dross, clinging, chang-ing and wasteful. It is merely a superficial covering.

   In Hebrew Scriptures, the ram was one of the various ani-mals used for sacrificial purposes, in this case by fire (which, as has already been indicated, is a major gate of purification).

7. SEALSKINS: This item is rendered as badgerskins in most Christian/English translations of Hebrew Scriptures which we consider to be incorrect.

   The metaphysical aspects of the colorations of the sealskin indicate an indigo washed with greenish-yellow, or orange-scarlet. Indigo represents the hue of the sky at sunrise and sunset.

The skin of the seal (whether or not heavily furred, but all the same, quite water-resistant), is highly reflective, especially when wet. Imagery evoked by seals includes, in the negative sense, indolence or laziness, a tendency to be indiscriminate, and deafness. In the positive sense, they indicate resilience and the ability to transcend environments.

8. WOOD: Trees are archetypal symbols of the link between heaven and earth, and share much common imagery with mankind. In this particular scriptural story, the wood that is described comes from the Acacia tree (Hebrew plural "Shittim"), one of the 15 trees identified in Hebrew Scriptures. The Acacia is renowned for its large thorns, which makes it difficult to approach, and its distinctive bouquet; a pleasant natural addition to honey in areas where bees frequent its yellow flowers.

The Hebrew symbols that comprise the singular word for the Acacia tree, "Shittah" שִׁטָּה (shin teth hé), are associated with the following colours: glowing orange, scarlet and vermillion, tinted with bright pale yellow and sky blue, overlaid on a background of deep warm olive and rich brown.

Positive metaphysical aspects of wood include adaptability, flexibility, stability, calm, quiet and virgin. Negatives are derived from the fact that wood may be shaped by man into idols and missile-like weapons (spears, javelins, bow and arrows). Its hardness evokes further meanings of something that is stiff and unyielding at the core.

A tree's cylindrical shape along with its inner growth rings are a gnostic symbol of the eternal circular pattern of incarnation and reincarnation. Other metaphysical meanings of wood infer material existence, the world of nature and its gnostic reflection of the esoteric, and illusions to be cast off.

The archetypal tree of metaphysics is rooted in the void, yet manifests on earth, further reflecting the meditative spine and nerve centres.

It should be noted that linen, goats' hair, rams' skin, seal-skin and acacia wood are all derived from natural sources, found above the ground, but are shaped by man to their desired final form.

9. OIL & ANOINTING OIL: This offering symbolizes the oil of life - the vital fluid that renews, reanimates and regenerates the body. It is metaphysically associated with love, joy, and gladness.
The thought of love which is poured over all, making a perfect whole (or holy) is the significance of the special type of oil used for this purpose.

10. SPICES: As a preservative, stimulant and enhancer of flavour, spice symbolizes and reflects the imperishable self that lies within the perishable form of flesh. The spiritual enhances the material.

11. SWEET INCENSE: The positive aspects of incense lie in its pleasant, pleasurable, beautiful and benevolent nature. Incense may be metaphysically interpreted to indicate that which transmutes the material to the esoteric: a solid to a vapour, and form to non-form. Along with the foregoing there is a transcendence from the finite to the infinite, the analytical to the abstract. It points to an alteration and refinement of animal matter in the human being.
The negative aspects of incense include the connotation of one who is squeamish and altruistic (in the sense of one who is well-meaning, but misguided). It further points up the danger of an artificial sense-perception of truth by oneself, which may in turn be transferred to others.

Again, oil, spices and sweet incense are derived from natural plant substances, but require man's ability to discard the dross through refinement. Also note that the preceding encompass the first 10 gifts or offerings that are described in the Scriptural passage. Three are derived from mineral resources, three from animal sources, and four from vegetation.

12. BREASTPLATE STONES: There are 12 stones, including onyx that are mentioned. Just as gemstones are cut from raw minerals to various geometric shapes and polished to obtain their desired final form, they reflect man's ability to change through polishing and cutting. Their geometric significance illustrates that they are symbols and reflectors of time and space, non-time and non- space.

All the items to be offered are encompassed by a four-part division that invariably leads to an elevation in one's state of consciousness at the completion of each ensuing stage.

The esoteric aspects of the construction of the Temple in the Wilderness have a deeper significance than can be covered in a book of this size. As has been indicated, it contains a plethora of major themes, one of which is the transcendence of the individual to a balanced awareness through love and compassion, wisdom and understanding. This leads to true peace within oneself, which in turn reflects to the outer world. The Hebrew Scriptural guidepost of T'rumah תרומה — of "every man whose heart maketh him willing" — is a metaphysical exclamation mark that directs one on an internal voyage of self-discovery and self-refinement.

The furnishings of the actual Temple, its framework and coverings (which are described in the verses from EX XXV: 9, onward) carry a more comprehensive metaphysical unfolding for the study and practice of purifying one's state of consciousness.

The Ancient Hebrew Sages used the theme of a willing heart that is open and free from fear to illuminate an idea of inner transcendence and peace. In so doing they evoked images of animate and inanimate objects, frequently utilizing colours to symbolize conditions of states of consciousness and conditions of energies. One will note that no quantities are mentioned, and that the actual Temple that is to be built is a portable one; it is not confined to one place in space or any particular moment in time.

They sought to symbolize an ideal spiritual entity that can be self-realized by all who endeavor to give with a truly free and willing heart.

The metaphysical exploration, combined with appropriate meditations, and guided by an experienced, physical teacher who has actually done the work, are the essence of Gnostic Hebrew Qabbal study and practice.

Bibliography

Achad, Frater. *Q.B.L. or the Brides Reception.* New York: Samuel
Weiser, 1974.
— *The Anatomy of the Body of God.* New York: Weiser, 1973.
— *The Egyptian Revival.* New York: Samuel Weiser Inc., 1969.
Albertus, Frater. *The Seven Rays of the Q.B.L.* York Beach, Maine:
Samuel Weiser Inc., 1967.
Alcalay, Reuben. *The Complete English-Hebrew Dictionary.* 2 vols.
Tel-Aviv, Jerusalem, Israel: Massada Publishing Co., 1981.
— *The Complete Hebrew-English Dictionary.* Tel-Aviv, Jerusalem,
Israel: Massada Publishing Co., 1981.
Bakktiar, Laleh. *Sufi, expressions of the mystic quest.* London:
Thames and Hudson, 1976.
Barnstone, Willis. English versions & trans. *The poems of Saint
John of the Cross.* New York: New Directions Books, 1972.
Blair, Lawrence. *Rythems of Visions.* New York: Shocken Books,
1976.
Blofeld, John. trans. & ed. *Tantric Mysticism of Tibet.* New York:
E.P. Dutton, 1970.
Buber, Martin. *I and Thou.* New York: Charles Scribners Sons,
1970.
— *Tales of the Hasidim.* New York: Shocken Books, 1974.

— *The Prophetic Faith*. New York: Macmillan, 1949.

Buddahdasa Bikkhu. *Anapanasati (Mindfulness of Breathing)*. Bangkok, Thailand: Sublime Life Mission, 1971/76.

Case, Foster Paul. *The True & Invisible Rosicrucian Order*. York Beach, Maine: Samuel Weiser, 1985.

Chang, C.D. Garma. trans. & annotator. *Teachings of Tibetan Yoga*. New Hyde Park, New York: University Books, 1963.

Chaysentier, Louis. *The Mysteries of Chartres Cathedral*. Wellingborough, England: Thorsons Publishers, 1972.

Chia, Mantak. *Awaken Healing Energy through the Tao*. New York: Aurora Press, 1983.

Chomsky, William. *Hebrew: The Eternal Language*. Philadelphia, Pa.: The Jewish Publication Society of America, 1957.

Cirlot, J.E. *A Dictionary of Symbols* – English Translation. London: Routledge & Regan Paul Ltd., 1962.

Cohen, A., Dr., M.A., Ph.D., D.H.L., ed. *Chronicles I&II*. London: The Soncino Press, 1952.

— *Daniel, Ezra, Nehemia*. London: The Soncino Press, 1951.

— *Ezekiel*. London: The Soncino Press, 1950.

— *Isaiah*. London: The Soncino Press, 1949.

— *Jeremiah*. London: The Soncino Press, 1949.

— *Job*. London: The Soncino Press, 1946.

— *Joshua & Judges*. London: The Soncino Press, 1950.

— *Kings I&II*. London: The Soncino Press, 1950.

— *Proverbs*. London: The Soncino Press, 1946.

— *Samuel I&II*. London: The Soncino Press, 1949.

— *The Five Megilloth*. London: The Soncino Press, 1946.

— *The Psalms*. London: The Soncino Press, 1945.

— *The Soncino Chumash*. London: The Soncino Press, 1947.

— *The Twelve Prophets*. London: The Soncino Press, 1948.

Collected Works, *Hebrew-English Lexicon of the Bible*. New York: Shicken Books, 1975.

Cozort, Daniel. *Highest Yoga Tantra*. Ithaca, NY: Snow Lion Publications, 1986.

Critchlow, Keith. *Order in Space*. London: Thames & Hudson, 1969.

Daczi, Gyorgy. *The Power of Limits*. Boulder Co.: Shambhala Publications, 1981.

Davies, Powell A. *The Meaning of the Dead Sea Scrolls*. New York: New American Library, 1956.

Delaforce, Gaetan. *The Templar Tradition*. Threshold Books, 1987.

Dimont, Max J. *The Indestructable Jews*. New York: New American Library, 1971.

Dobin, Joel C., Rabbi. *To Rule Both Day & Night*. New York: Inner Traditions International, 1977.

Douglas, Nik & White, Meryl. comp. *Karmapa, The Black Hat Lama of Tibet*. London: Luzac & Company, 1976.

Dourley, John P. *The Psyche as Sacrament*. Toronto: Inner City Books, 1981.

Dreher, Diane. *The Tao of Inner Peace*. Harper Perennial, 1991.

Eliade, Mircea. *The Myth of the Eternal Return*. Princeton, NJ: Princeton University Press, 1954.

Emerson, Ralph Waldo. *Essays*. New York: Harper Colophon Books.

Epstein, Perle. *Kabbalah, the way of the Jewish mystic*. New York: Samuel Weiser Inc., 1979.

Flanagan, Pat G. *Pyramid Power*. Glendale, Col.: Pyramid Publishers, 1973.

Fox, Emmett. *The Sermon on the Mount*. New York: Harper & Row, 1938.

Friedman, Irving, trans. & commentary. *Book of Creation, Sepher Yetzirah*. New York: Samuel Weiser Inc., 1977.

Friedman, Richard Elliott. *Who Wrote the Bible?* New York: Summit Books, 1987.

Ghyka, Matila. *The Geometry of Art & Life*. New York: Dover Publications, 1977.

Glazerson, M. *Sparks of the Holy Tongue*. New York: Feldheim Publishers, 1975.

Godeven, David. *Godeven's Cabalistic Encyclopedia*, 1979.

Goodman, Philip. *The Passover Anthology*. The Jewish Publication Society of America, 1966.

Govinda, Anagarika Lama. *Foundations of Tibetan Mysticism.* York Beach, Maine: Samuel Weiser Inc.

Graves, Robert, Potai, Raphael. *Hebrew Myths, the Book of Genesis.* New York: Doubleday, 1964.

Graves, Robert. *The White Goddess.* London: Faher and Faher Limited, 1961.

Greenstein, George. *Frozen Star.* New York: Freundlich Books, 1983.

Gribbin, John. *In Search of Schrodingers Cat.* New York: Bantam, 1984.

Gurdjieff, G.I. *Beelzebub's Tales to His Grandson.* Books #2 & #3. New York: E.P. Dutton, 1973.

Gyatso, Geshe Kelsang. *Clear Light of Bliss.* London: Wisdom Publications, 1982.

Haeller, Stephan A. *The Gnostic Jung.* Wheaton Ill.: Quest Books, 1982.

Halevi, Z'ev ben Shimon. *Kabbalah and Exodus.* Boulder, Col.: Shambhala Publications Inc., 1980.

Hall, Manley P. *Death to Rebirth.* Los Angeles: Philosophical Research Society, 1979.

— *Freemasonry of the Ancient Egyptians.* Los Angeles: Philosophical Research Society, 1971.

— *Reincarnation.* Los Angeles: Philosophical Research Society, 1946.

— *The Secret Teachings of All Ages.* Los Angeles: Philosophical Research Society, 1975, #2424.

— *Old Testament Wisdom.* Los Angeles: The Philosophical Research Society Inc., 1957.

Hambidge, Jay. *The Elements of Dynamic Symmetry.* New York: Dover, 1967.

Heninger, S.K. Jr. *Touches of Sweet Harmony.* San Marino, CA: The Huntington Library, 1974.

Hirsch, Raphael Samson, Rabbi. trans. & commentary. *The Psalms.* Jerusalem, Israel, New York: Feldheim Publishers, 1978.

Hodgson, Joan. *Astrology, the sacred science.* Hampshire, England: The White Eagle Publishing Trust, 1978.

Hoover, Thomas. *Zen Culture.* New York: Vintage Books, 1978.

Idel, Moshe. *The Mystical Experience in Abraham Abulafia.* New York: State University of New York Press, 1988.

Joseph, Akiba ben. *The Book of Formation.* New York: KATV Publishing House Inc., 1970.

Jung, C.G. *Mandala Symbolism.* Princeton: Bollingen Series, 1972.

— *Modern Man in Search of his Soul.* New York: Harcourt Brace Jovanovich, 1933 (orig. printing)

— *On the Nature of the Psyche.* Princeton: Bollingen Series, 1969.

— *Psychology and the Occult.* Bollingen, University of Princeton Press, 1977.

— *Psychology and Western Religion.* Bollingen, University of Princeton Press, 1984.

— "Symbols & Transformation." *Collected Works,* vol. 5. Princeton: Bollingen Series, 1956.

Kaplan, Aryeh, trans., intro., commentary. *The Bahir.* New York: Samuel Weiser, 1979.

— *Meditation and Kabbalah.* New York: Samuel Weiser, 1982.

—. *Meditation and the Bible.* New York: Samuel Weiser, 1978.

Kapleau, Philip Roshi. *The Three Pillars of Zen.* New York: Anchor Books, Doubleday, 1989.

Kaufman, Yehezbel. *The Religion of Israel.* New York: Shoken Books, original 1937.

Kavanaugh, Kieran O.C.D. & Rodrigues, Otilio O.C.D. trans. *The Collected Works of St. John of the Cross,* I.C.S. Publications, Washington, D.C. 1979.

Kavanaugh, Kieran O.C.D. trans. *The Collected Works of St. Teresa of Avila.* Vol. II. Washington, D.C.: I.C.S. Publications, 1980.

Keller, Werner. *The Bible as History.* London: Hodder & Stoughton, 1967.

Kenner, Hugh. *Bucky, a guided tour of Buckminster Fuller.* New York: William Morrow & Company Inc., 1973.

Knight, Gareth. *A Practical Guide to Qabalistic Symbolism.* New York: Samuel Weiser, 1978.

Krishnamurti, J. *Exploration into Insight.* San Francisco: Harper & Row, 1980.

— *Freedom from the Known.* New York: Harper & Row, 1969.

Kushner, Lawrence. *Honey from the Rock.* San Francisco: Harper
& Row, 1983.

— *The River of Light.* San Francisco: Harper & Row, 1981.

La Berge, Stephen, Ph.D. *Lucid Dreaming.* New York: Ballantine,
1986.

Lado, Lama. *Bardo Teachings.* Ithaca, N.Y.: Snow Lion
Publications, 1987.

Legget, Trevor. *A First Zen Reader.* Rutland, Vt., Tokyo: Charles
E. Tuttle Company, 1960.

Levenson, Jon D. *Sinai & Lion.* San Francisco: Harper & Row,
1987.

Levi, Eliphas. *The Great Secret.* New York: Samuel Weiser Inc.

— *The Mysteries of the Qabalah.* New York: Samuel Weiser Inc.

Love, Jeff. *The Quantum Gods.* Wiltshire, England: Compton
Russell Ltd., 1976.

Luzzatto, Moses C., Rabbi. *General Principles of the Kabbalah.*
New York: Samuel Weiser Inc., dist., 1970.

Maimonides, Moses. *The Guide for the Perplexed.* New York:
Dover, 1956.

Mathers, S.L. MacGregor. *The Kabbalah Unveiled.* London:
Routledge & Kegon Paul Ltd., 1957.

Mathews, Boris. trans. *The Herder Symbol Dictionary.* Wilmette,
Illinois: Chiron Publications, 1986.

Mendel, Nisson. *Rabbi Schneur Zalman.* Kehot Publication
Society, 1974.

— *Metaphysical Bible Dictionary.* Unity Vill., MO: Unity School of
Christianity, 1931.

— *Metaphysics* Vol. I&II. Unity Village, MA: Unity Church for
Religious Studies.

Michell, John. *City of Revelation.* London: Abacus, 1973.

— *The View over Atlantis.* London: Abacus, 1973.

Mishna, Rammurti S., M.D. *The Textbook of Yoga Psychology.*
New York: The Julian Press Inc., 1971.

Munk, Michael L., Rabbi. *Wisdom in the Hebrew Alphabet.*
Brooklyn, New York: Mesorak Publications Ltd.

Needleman, Jacob, forward & compilation. *The Sword of Gnosis*. Baltimore, Maryland: Penguin Books, 1974.

Ouspensky, P.D. *The Fourth Way*. New York: Vintage Books.

Pagels, Elaine. *The Gnostic Gospels*. New York: Vintage Books, 1981.

Pagels, Heinz. R. *The Cosmic Code*. New York: Bantam, 1983.

Pennick, Nigel. *Sacred Geometry*. Wellingborough, England: Turnstone Press, 1980.

Ponce, Charles. *Kabbalah*. Wheaton, IL/Madras, India/London, England: Theosophical Publishing House, Quest Books, 1986.

Preserved and collated in the Coptic Museum, Old Cairo. *The Gospel According to Thomas*. New York: Harper & Tow, 1959.

Raleigh, A.S. Occult Geometry. Marina del Rey, CA: De Vorss and Company, 1981.

Rey, H.A. *The Stars*. Boston: Houghton, Mifflin Company, 1952.

Rinpoche, Kalu. *The Dharma*. New York: State University of New York Press, 1986.

Rinpoche, Namgyal. *Body, Speech and Mind*. Toronto: Crystal Staff Publications, 1983.

— *Glimmerings of the Mystical Life*. Toronto: Crystal Word Publications, 1983.

— *The Dome of Heaven*. Toronto: Namgyal House, 1983.

— *The Womb of Form*. Crystal Word Publications,

Robinson, James M. gen. ed. *The Nag Hammadi Library*. San Francisco: Harper & Row, 1981.

Roget, Peter Mark. *Roget's Thesaurus*. Great Britain: Longman Group Ltd. 1852 and 1962.

Rosenberg, Stuart E. *The Christian Problem, a Jewish View*. New York: Hippocrene Books, 1986.

Sagan, Carl. *Cosmos*. New York: Ballantine, 1985.

Sanford, John A. *The Invisible Partners*. New York: Paulist Press, 1980.

Scherman, Nasson, Zlotowitz Meir, Rabbis. gen. ed. *Tehillim – Psalms 1–150*, Vol. I&II. A traditional commentary. Brooklyn, NY: Mesorah Publications Ltd., 1985.

Schneerson, Menachem M. Rabbi. *On the Essence of Chassidus*.

Brooklyn, N.Y.: Kehot Publication Society, 1978.

Schneerson, Sholom Dov Ber Rabbi. *Kuntres Ama'ayon Mibais Hashem*. Brooklyn, N.Y.: Kehot Publication Society, 1969. trans. by Posner J. Zalman.

Scholem, Gershom C. *Jewish Gnosticism, Merkabah Mysticism and Talmudic Tradition*. New York: The Jewish Theological Seminary of America, 1960.

— *Kabbalah and its Symbolism*. New York: Schoken Books, 1969.

— *Kabbalah*. New York: New American Library, 1974.

— ed. *Zohar, The Book of Splendor*. New York: Schoken Books, 1949.

Schwaller de Lubicz, R.A. *Symbol and the Symbolic*. New York: Autumn Press, 1978.

— *The Temple in Man*. New York: Autumn Press Inc., 1977.

Sheinkin, David, M.D. *Path of the Kabbalah*. New York: Paragon House Publishers, 1986.

Sole-Leris, Amadeo. *Tranquility & Insight*. Boston, Mass.: Shambahala, 1986.

Stanley, Thomas. trans. *The Chaldean Oracles*. Gillette, New Jersey: Heptangle Books MCMLXXXIX.

Stryk, Lucien. intro. and commentary. *World of the Buddha*. New York: Grove Press Inc., 1968.

Suares, Carlo. *The Cipher of Genesis*. Boston, London: Shambala, 1970.

— *The Passion of Judas*. Berkeley & London: Shambhala, 1973.

— *The Resurrection of the Word*. Berkeley & London: Shambhala, 1975.

— *The Sepher Yetsira*. Boulder, Col.: Shambhala Publications Inc., 1976.

— *The Song of Songs*. Berkeley & London: Shambalah, 1972.

Szekely, Edmond Bordeaux. compared, ed. & trans. *The Essene Gospel of Truth*. Vol. I&II. International Biogenic Society, 1981.

— *The Gospel of the Essenes*. Walden, England: The C. Ul. Daniel Co. Ltd., 1976.

Taylor, Thomas. *The Theoretic Arithmetic of the Pythagoreans*. New York: Samuel Weiser, 1972.

— *New Jerusalem Bible, The* Garden City, NY: Doubleday, 1985.

— *Path of Freedom., The* Sri Lanka: Buddhist Publication Society, 1977.

— *Secret of the Golden Flower, The* New York, London: Harcourt Brace Jovanovich, 1962.

— *Tibetan Book of the Dead, The* Boulder, Co., London: Shambhala, 1975.

— *Zohar, The* Vol. I-V. London: The Soncino Press, 1978.

Tompkins, Peter. *Mysteries of the Great Pyramid.* New York, Harper & Row.

— *Mysteries of the Mexican Pyramids.* New York: Harper & Row, 1976.

— *The Magic of Obelisks.* New York: Harper & Row, 1981.

Trungpa, Chogyam & Fremantle, Francesca. trans. and commentary. *The Tibetan Book of the Dead.* Boulder, Co., London: Shambala Publications Inc., 1975.

Trungpa, Chogyam. *Cutting Through Spiritual Materialism.* Boulder, Co.: Shambhala Publications, 1973.

— *The Myth of Freedom.* Boulder, CO: Shambhala Publications, 1976.

— *The Myth of Freedom.* Boulder, CO, and London, England: Shambhala, 1973.

Underhill, Evelyn. *Practical Mysticism.* New York: E.P. Dutton, 1943.

Waite, A.E. *The Holy Kabbalah.* University Books/Citadel Press.

Watson, Lyall. *The Romeo Error.* London: Hodden & Stoughton Limited, 1974.

Weinberg, Steven. *The First Three Minutes.* New York: Bantam, 1977.

Wentz-Evans, W.Y. *Tibetan Yoga & Secret Doctrines.* London: Oxford University Press, 1958.

Wilheim, Richard. trans., Jung, C.G., commentator. *The Secret of the Golden Flower.* New York, London: Harcourt Brace Jovanovich, 1962.

— trans. *The I Ching.* Vol. I&II. Bollingen Series XIX, Princeton, N.J.: Princeton University Press, 1950.

Wilson, William. *New Wilson's Old Testament Studies.* Grand
Rapids, Michigan: Kregel Publications, 1987.

Winston, David. intro. and commentary. *The Wisdom of Solomon.*
New York: Doubleday, 1979.

Wong Ch'Ug Dor-je, Ninth Karmapa. *The Mahamudra.* Library
of Tibetan Works & Archives, 1978.

— *World of the Buddha.* Grove Press Inc., 1968.

Yadin, Yigael. *The Message of the Scrolls.* New York: Simon &
Schuster, 1957.

Young, Robert L.L.D. *Analytical Concordance to the Bible,* 22nd
Edition, revised. New York: Funk & Wagnalls.

Zaehner, R.C. *Hindu & Muslim Mysticism.* New York: Schoken
Books, 1969.

Zalman, Schneur Rabbi. *Likuth Amarim.* Tanya Slavita 1796 –
Zalkiev 1798.

— *Philosophy of Chabad.* Brooklyn, NY: Kehot Publication
Society, 1980.

Zlotowitz, Meir Rabbi and Scherman, Nasson Rabbi. commen-
taries and allegorical translation. *Song of Songs.* Brooklyn, NY:
Mesorah Publications Ltd., 1977.

Zodhiates, Spiro, Th.D. *The Hebrew-Greek Key Study Bible.*
Chattanooga, Tn., 1984.

— *Zohar, from the In the Beginning.* New York: Concord Grove
Press, 1983.

Collophon

The text is set in 12 point Adobe Garamond, Adobe Garamond Expert and Hebraica fonts. Following the instructions in the text, the drawings were created using Aldus FreeHand as the drawing instrument. Layout was in QuarkXPress 3.3 on a Macintosh Quadra 950 and output to an Agfa Avantra imagesetter.

The editor was Laurie Willberg; typographic design, cover and execution of drawings by Morley Chalmers.